BONKERS FOR CONKERS
A British street game that became an International competition
& other true stories

PAULINE NEVINS

COPYRIGHT

The majority of these essays first appeared in slightly
different form, and often with a different title, as
newspaper columns in the Northern California
newspapers the *Auburn Journal* and *The Union*.

Cover photograph of Oliver (Oli) Wheatley by permission
of St.John Burkett
Organising Committee,
World Conker Championships.

Cover design by Laurie Barrows
lauriebarrows.com

THANK YOU NOTES~~

To my husband, Jim, for reading everything I write, and for laughing in all the right places;

To my daughter, Tina, without whose adventurous spirit I would have much less to write about;

To my editor, Gloria Beverage, for her expertise, encouragement and friendship;

To my son, Aaron, for sharing his creative expertise;

To members of my two writers' groups:
Coffee, Tea and Saki: Barbara, Bill N., Bill S., Dick, Donna and Miyoko, for their lasting friendships and ongoing encouragement;
The Auburn Gold Country Writers for providing valuable resources, education and support;

And to family and friends whose enthusiastic praise of my memoir inspired me to keep writing.

CONTENTS

INTRODUCTION

It was only after I retired and hopped off the hamster wheel that I took time to attend a memoir writing course given at a local community college. My daughter, Tina, had enjoyed hearing stories about my childhood in England—a mixed-race child growing up in a chaotic Irish family—and encouraged me to write them down.

During the last day of the memoir class a sheet of yellow lined paper was circulated by one of the students. The heading read: "Are you interested in a writers' group?"

Twelve years later our group of seven are still meeting—writing, reading, critiquing and supporting each other. It is the six members of this writers' group that I credit with providing the encouragement I needed to call myself a writer, and have the nerve to publish a memoir: *"Fudge" the Downs and Ups of a Biracial, Half-Irish British War Baby*.

Many of the responses to my memoir from family, friends and others in the United States and England were so touching that they made me cry.

The book's publication spurred events I never imagined. I was interviewed on three television stations: Terry Fay on Lake Wildwood's Channel 95

Susan Rushton on Auburn's community television, and Lori and Melissa on Channel 31's *Good Day Sacramento*. I was invited to speak at book clubs and appear at book fairs. At first I was nervous when I attended these events, but my confidence grew and they became stimulating and fun.

With my memoir published I had time to focus on other forms of writing. One of the writers' group members encouraged me to submit a story to *The Union*, a newspaper published in an adjacent county. I've included the column in this collection: *You Say 'tomayto and I say tomahto.'*

Now there was no stopping me. I submitted a different column to the *Auburn Journal*, my local paper. Richard Hanner was the paper's editor at the time and he published my work, said some nice things about my writing, and encouraged me to send in pieces more often.

Susan Rushton, who interviewed me on her *Ah Muse!* television program, is also a long-time columnist for the *Auburn Journal*. She has published a book: "And Another Thing...Reflections from My Small Town" —a collection of her newspaper columns. Susan's volume inspired me to publish this book.

I hope you enjoy these personal essays, and that my experience encourages you to explore your creative urges. It's never too late!

Market Street, Wellingborough—circa 1970
Photograph from *Wellingborough Memories* by
Joyce and Maurice Palmer

WHEN I WAS YOUNG

*My hometown of Wellingborough is in a
geographic area known as the East Midlands. The
town was granted a royal market charter in 1201 by
King John.*

*When I was growing up there, a market was held
twice a week—on Wednesdays and Saturdays.
Vendors' stalls filled the market square in the shade of*

1

All Hallows Parish Church. Wellingborough has had several growth spurts. The one I remember occurred in the 1960s when a large population from London—known as the London overspill—descended on our small town. Some attribute the destruction of many of the town's historic buildings with this increase in population. Whatever the cause, the town changed forever.

*The stories "**Bonkers for Conkers**," "**The Great Escapes**," "**Getting the Boot**," and "**Shillings and Pence**," are entwined in memories of the Wellingborough that I knew.*

Bonkers for Conkers

August 25, 2016

I'm not sure I would have survived my chaotic childhood if it were not for street games, and a neighborhood of same-age kids with whom to play them. The girls skipped rope, played hopscotch in the chalk squares outside front gates, or two-ball—singing rhymes while juggling balls as they bounced against the outside wall of their brick houses.

In the summer the boys played cricket in the park across the street, and switched to football in the winter. In the Autumn, conkers consumed every English boy's waking moments.

Conkers may not be familiar to most Americans, but every British boy who once ran the streets in short trousers has played the game. Each boy would face off against another lad, dangling the toxic seed from a Horse Chestnut tree—the conker—from a 12-inch piece of string.

In autumns long past, my three young brothers and their friends would scramble through wet fields near the English village where we lived to collect these conkers—solid, dark-brown seeds the size of walnuts. Green prickly pods lay cracked open beside the seeds they once protected.

Using a stone and a nail the boys busied themselves hammering a hole in the center of the conkers through which they threaded a length of string, which was knotted at one end. Ready for battle. A penny toss decided which of the two competitors would strike, and which would receive. The receiver would hold his conker at arm's length. The striker would wrap his conker string around one hand leaving enough length to flick his conker at his opponent's. After three unsuccessful attempts to bash his opponent's conker to bits, the striker became the receiver.

Players battled until someone's conker was destroyed. The winning conker earned a point, and was named a "oner." If the smashed conker had previously crushed one conker (was a oner), then the winning conker was awarded that point and became a "twoer" — and so on.

It was a transatlantic chat with my brother, Kevan, that triggered the conker memories.

"Did you know Dick Swailes?"

Not waiting for my response Kevan went on. "Well, he was driving by the Shuckburgh Arms in Southwick (a village 30 miles away), when he saw the advertisement for a conker championship. They hold one every October in the pub's beer garden. Well, Dick parked his van and registered. Then guess what?" Kevan went on, his voice rising, "He ended up winning the championship!" We both laughed. "They gave him a trophy and a weird crown with conkers stuck all over it."

Curious to learn more, I checked out the World Conker Championship's website. I learned the event had its start in 1965 when lads at a local pub turned to a game of conkers when torrential rain postponed their fishing trip. Over the next fifty years this impromptu game ballooned into a highly-organized international event generating thousands of pounds for charity. Competitors from as far afield as Sri Lanka and Mexico have descended on the picturesque village of Southwick. Even the United States sent a contingent—a team from Wisconsin. Their cheesy headgear was explained to BBC News online: "We're from the cheese state."

There were never any organized conker contests when I was a kid. I wondered if school children still played the game. "Not anymore," I learned from Trevor, a visitor from England. Then he added with a sarcastic chuckle, "The Health and Safety people are afraid somebody will get injured."

This reputation of the Institution of Health and Safety as an over-protective party pooper is so pervasive the organization felt compelled to prove they weren't killjoys. They sponsored a team in the conker competition. Ray Hurst, the Institute's president, told the UK Telegraph, "We like to have fun like anyone else. You just have to manage the risks, not ban them into oblivion."

The opposite of obscurity was on the mind of John Doyle, the 2014 conker champion. He suggested to the BBC that the game be elevated. "There's a lot more strategy involved than in other games. Hopefully it'll be in the Olympics next time."

Achieving Mr. Doyle's Olympic goal will take some doing. The illustrious World Conker Championship is included on the list of "12 Brilliant (But Bonkers) Competitions in Britain," posted online by Trip Adviser.

The conker contest keeps company with the Christmas Pudding Relay Race in Dorset; the Custard Pie Championship in Kent, where contestants throw pies with their non-dominant hand—maximum points for hits to the face. And my husband's favorite, the Oxford Pram Race where a friend is pushed in a baby carriage for 2/3 of a mile with mandatory breaks at 7 pubs—each downing a pint at every stop.

I'd read that poor conker harvests and gale-force winds have cancelled games in the past, so out of curiosity I called Tom, the landlord of the Shuckburgh Arms.

"Are the games on this year?" I asked. I had no intention of attending but hoped my brother would. Tom said as of now the contest was on. He invited me to come to Southwick, a village of less than 200, and join the expected horde of 3-4,000 visitors.

"Although I'm not sure where everyone is staying," he said with a chuckle. "Anyway, you could come for the beer and stay for the conkers."

****

The Great Escapes

February 3, 2017

My nephew Richard's Facebook post reminded me there once was a zoo in the center of our hometown in the East Midlands. The zoo was owned by the town's pet shop owner, John Stevens. It started with his private collection of exotic animals that roamed the grounds of his Croyland Gardens estate before he opened the zoo in 1943. For sixpence, locals could wander around the zoo all day and forget there was a war going on.

Richard's Facebook post included a link to a Pathe news website. Before everyone owned a television, cinemas were packed with people watching Pathe's black and white newsreels. These reports covered everything from catastrophes to peculiar events in the lives of ordinary people.

This particular newsreel, Richard wrote, featured his Uncle Morris, one of the zoo keepers. I'd heard of Morris, but had never met him, let alone knew he had worked at the zoo. I also didn't know this film existed. It was made at a time when I was a teenager focused on important things like perfecting my eyeliner and backcombing my hair.

The newsreel opened with Morris and his wife and daughter sitting by their fireside, each engrossed in reading a newspaper.

The narrator began with, "Home isn't home without a fireside pet... and Morris likes to bring the little chap home for the evening."

Sprawled in front of the fire is Simba the lion. He didn't look very little to me.

Simba was the one that let out the roars that caused me and my teenage girlfriends to scream in fright, and then scream again with laughter, as we teetered passed the zoo at night in our stiletto heels.

The film's narrator goes on to say it's a lovely evening for an outing, and out the door goes Morris and Simba. With the lion sitting in the front passenger seat of the Morris Minor Van, he drove to the village of Isham for a pint. The pub is named— what else? The Red Lion.

Morris and Simba are shown entering the front door of the pub. Several roars are heard and five men scamper out of the pub's back door. Simba bellies up to the bar and guzzles a "Double Wellingborough," the local brew poured by the landlord Fred Noble.

After watching the newsreel I wondered what else went on at the zoo. I was entertained for hours reading *Zoo Memories* on the local council's website. There was a sea lion that managed to find its way out of the zoo and flapped its way into the local brook before being captured. Two penguins ended up half a mile from the zoo in Justine Pearce's garden. Their freedom was also short-lived. They were captured after one night on the lam by Justine's father and a neighbor who managed to coax the duo into a box. The penguins had been spotted the night before waddling down Croyland Road. The motorist who reported them to the police was advised to go home or risk being breathalyzed.

Another story, chronicled by Jean Knight, described her visit to the zoo one afternoon.

Jean, and her friend Gladys, had a half day off from work and were strolling around the zoo enjoying an ice cream cornet when they heard someone shout that a monkey had escaped. Next thing Jean knew her "ice cream went flying" and she was "taken in a strong hairy grip." Boo Boo, a large chimpanzee, had taken her hostage.

The chimp dragged Jean out of the zoo, with her friend Gladys and a gang of zoo goers in pursuit, screaming. Up Sheep Street Jean was pulled passed my favorite place, The Hind Hotel, where tipsy customers cheered them on. Across Market Street they went just as patrons were filing out of the matinee showing of "Tarzan and Jane" at the Regal Cinema. Must be a publicity stunt? More cheers from onlookers.

Boo Boo the chimp wasn't familiar enough with the town to stay away from the Midland Road police station. He was finally apprehended—snagged in a large net by several Bobbies. The zoo consoled Jean with a replacement ice cream cornet.

As you can imagine, these episodes hardly boosted the zoo's reputation. They were already in trouble with the Royal Society for the Prevention of Cruelty to Animals. And there were other problems. The zoo was losing money and facing foreclosure.

On my last visit to my hometown a couple of years ago I walked the block from The Hind Hotel and down Sheep Street to where the zoo had been. All that remains is a brick wall, a bronze plaque and ...memories.

****

Getting the Boot

April 13, 2017

If you'd grown up in my hometown in England before the 1970s your educational future would've been decided before age twelve. A mandatory written exam, known as the 'eleven plus' (named for the approximate age of the students) determined whether you were either college material, or you were not. I was not.

At age 15, after completing four years at a school that taught the basics, I was destined to join the rest of my blue collar neighbors in the windowless world of shoe manufacturing. Factory work was plentiful back then. I could quit work one day and find another job the next. This flitting around would have stopped had I stayed in England instead of scampering off to America. In the late 70s, centuries-old manufacturing companies were closing in droves in Northamptonshire, the heart of the U.K's boot and shoe industry. The importing of cheap goods, and the exporting of jobs, were blamed. Tastes changed as well. Fewer people were wearing smart leather boots and shoes.

During this downturn, the factory of W.J. Brooks Ltd., owned by a Mr. Steve Pateman, and located in Earls Barton—just a few miles from my hometown—was also in trouble. Sales of his quality leather brogues had declined to the point the factory was about to close.

"It was a random phone call from a woman from a fetish shoe shop in Folkstone," quoted *The Chronicle and Echo*, " who asked Steve if he could supply her with ladies' shoes in men's sizes." The niche market of erotic footwear had opened up. "Kinky boots" became all the rage—thigh-high boots reinforced with metal to support a man's weight. The product saved the factory. Although Steve worried the locals would disapprove, he was more concerned about keeping his factory open and his employees working. He didn't hesitate to do whatever it took. A company brochure was in the works, but none of his employees would model the boots. Steve, a stocky rugby player, ended up shaving his own legs for the photo shoot.

You can imagine what a national stir it caused to have a venerable manufacturer go from making conservative brogues to stiletto-heeled boots—for men. The story was dramatic enough to inspire a BBC documentary called, "Trouble at the Top;" followed by a British comedy-drama, "Kinky Boots;" and a Broadway musical by the same name that earned 13 Tony nominations and claimed 6 awards.

All I can say is, it was a good job Steve's factory didn't employ me. It might have gone under even with the kinky boots franchise. One of my first shoe factory jobs was operating a machine called a skiver. My task was to shave off enough leather from the upper part of a shoe section so the machinist could stitch it to the lower section. If I didn't take off enough leather the upper would be too thick for the machinists' needle. If I took too much off, holes would appear. I was inept. I consistently skived off too much leather creating more waste than anyone in the factory. The foreman, the only male in the building, fired me. I was holding my last weekly pay packet, and crying when a co-worker and neighbor, Marian Shaw, asked me what happened. She marched straight over to the foreman.

"You can't give Pauline the sack. If you do, we're all out."

During this time, "The Rag Trade" was one of the most popular sitcoms on British television. The comedy series featured the antics of women working in a clothing factory. The shop steward, Paddy Fleming, was the show's star. In response to labor disputes ranging from the minor to the miniscule, Paddy would blow an ear-piercing blast from a whistle whipped from the pocket of her smock. These shrill alerts would be followed by her declaring, "Everybody out," a work stoppage catch-phrase that swept the country. These escapades drove Reg Turner, the sitcom's foreman, off his rocker.

It was against this backdrop that my loyal neighbor, Marian Shawn, made her threat of a factory strike. The foreman relented and rehired me. The following week, I got bored and quit.

I would eventually become "college material" and achieve my dream of getting a degree. It just had to wait until I reached America.

****

Shillings and Pence

February 1, 2018

The England of my childhood has changed, a realization that hit as I watched Mary Berry and Paul Hollywood, judges on the Great British Bake Off show, demonstrate the preparation of a "foolproof" buche de Noel—a Christmas Log.

My confusion began with the ingredients, which were given in metrics. England used the imperial system when I was growing up. Liters, meters and grams mean nothing to me. Adding to my frustration, internet calculators gave varying conversions. Then there was the oven temperature: 200 degrees I called to my husband from the kitchen.

"How can you cook anything at 200 degrees?"

"Maybe it's a British gas oven number," he answered.

I thought he could be right, although he was focused on a football game and would have said anything to keep me quiet. But I managed to create a chocolate log that resembled that of the British Bake Off duo. My task would've been easier, though, had those measurements been anything but metric.

I didn't like how England had changed. I thought the Brexit mob was off their rockers to leave the European Union, but now I see why some were struggling with an altered country. And it isn't only pints, ounces and miles that have gone by the wayside. The money is also different.

The United Kingdom adopted a decimal currency on Feb.15, 1971. The date was labeled "D-Day" for Decimal Day—the same designation given for the Allied invasion of Normandy in World War II, if you can believe that.

In the United States, Congress got involved in the metric debate around the same time Britain was converting, but they bumped up against anti-big government forces. To date, the United States, Liberia, and Myanmar are the only three countries in the world that have not converted to metric, although the U.S. is part-way there. I see liters written on wine and water bottles, and runners compete in kilometer races that I have to convert to miles to appreciate their achievements.

When I visited England nine years after the money changed, I was so confused that I held out a handful of coins to shopkeepers so they could take what they needed. I might as well have been in Bangladesh.

I don't recognize any of the British money. The sweet little farthing, Britain's smallest coin both in size and value, fell out of favor ten years before D-Day. The silver sixpence, the brass twelve-sided threepenny bit, and the royal sounding half-crown have hit the dust bin.

The one coin I'm not sorry to see go is the penny. This coin was the size of a pancake and is credited with ruining tons of trouser pockets. With the penny and the farthing gone, how will young people get the connection between the old money and the penny-farthing bicycle, as my generation did? The silver shilling was also kicked off the island. Worth 12 pennies, it was replaced by a coin worth five pee. Yes, pee. Originally the new money was to be called "new pence," but morphed into 'p'.

The shilling holds a special place in my memory. Like every home in our neighborhood of attached brick houses with sooty chimney pots, our utilities were supplied on a pay-as-you-go basis. An electric meter was housed in a small cupboard by the front bay window and a gas meter mounted in the creepy cupboard space under the stairs. Shillings inserted into the electric meter would keep the lights on. A shilling in the gas meter would keep the stove going.

When Mother wasn't pushing me out of the backdoor to borrow shillings from the neighbors, never to be repaid, I was taught the art of coin counterfeiting.

My Irish stepfather, Harry, who never shied away from any illegal act that could get the better of the British, initiated my education. A copper ha'penny (half-penny), was worth one twenty-fourth of a shilling, and was only slightly larger. With the aid of a large, rusting metal rasp, Harry, taught my other siblings and me how to file down the ha'penny small enough to be inserted into the meter slot meant for shillings.

When the gas and the electric man came to empty out meters, he'd separate the few shillings from the pile of filed-down ha'pennies, and stack them in neat rows on the living room table. Unlike the neighbors who received money back—having paid for more utilities than they used—Mother received a solemn shake of the head and a bill.

In one of her letters, my mother wrote complaining that the British government hadn't bothered to check with the people before changing the money. The U.S. supporters of a metric conversion may have done well to emulate the Brits, employing the adage,

"It's easier to get forgiveness than it is to get permission."

"We have always found the Irish a bit odd.
They refuse to be English."
Winston Churchill

MUM AND SID

One of my mother's favorite, but oh so depressing mantras was "better the hell you know than the hell you don't know." This fear that any change from current misery could result in worse misery kept my mother cemented in a relationship with an Irish man who did an excellent job of displaying every ugly stereotype attributed to the Irish male: He was a drunkard, violent and lazy.

Mother needed an ally to leave "the old man" as we called him. She found one in Sid, a quiet English accountant.

The stories, "The Wearing of the Green," and "What Kept Ye?" are from the time before Sid made the confusing decision to take on Mother and eight kids. "Right and Left," and "Furry Friend or Foe," let you in on Mother and Sid's relationship. "Many Happy Returns" is a present to my mother.

The Wearing of the Green

March 25, 2018

D id Your Mother Come from Ireland?" goes the first line in the song by Jimmy Kennedy—inspired by a question overheard on a train to Dublin.

Like millions of Irish, my mother emigrated. She lived for more than fifty years in England where she gave birth to eight children in as many years. I popped out in the middle—a dark-skinned souvenir donated by an American serviceman. This was war-torn England, a time when homesick soldiers were comforted by more than tea and crumpets.

In addition to doing her part for the war effort, Mother enjoyed criticizing the Royal Family, placing a sixpenny bet on a Sunday horserace, and puffing away on her Woodbine cigarettes. She was addicted, I realize now. At times, the strike of her match would awaken me before the sun rose.

Mother's half brother, my Uncle Jim O'Toole, had also emigrated and lived a bachelor's life in London—less than two hours away by train. Every visit he carried a battered leather suitcase with the middle tied with string and stuffed with clothes for Mother to wash. Uncle Jim would always ask me to iron his laundered shirts. He chose me, an 8-year-old, over my two older half sisters.

The flat iron was heated on the gas stove in the kitchen. To test the temperature, I'd turn the iron upside down, and spit on the bottom—just like Mother did. But unlike my mother, I couldn't judge the iron's heat, which meant I would end up scorching Uncle Jim's shirts. Scrubbing the collars only worsened the brown streaks; my dripping tears didn't help. When my uncle got ready to leave, he would press into my hand a half-a-crown—worth two shillings and sixpence. Hadn't he seen those shirts, I wondered? I knew he'd want his money back if he had. But, he didn't. What's more, the next time he came to visit, he again asked me to iron his shirts.

Between my uncle's visits, we'd make room for lodgers. There were nights when unfamiliar voices drifted upstairs. In the morning I'd kick away the rubber hot water bottle, now cold, and push off the coats Mother had piled on the bed to keep my sisters and me warm. I'd shiver my way downstairs praying the coal fire was lit and curious to know what face would appear from under the rumpled covers on the living room couch.

"Top of the mornin'" was the usual greeting. My stepfather, Harry, had brought another grateful young Irishman home from the pub.

At times we'd have as many as three Irish lodgers, thirteen people sharing one bath, and one toilet, an inconvenience I credit with expanding the size of my bladder. I still remember some of their names. There was Gus, who after taking his Friday night bath, slipped on the cement floor and knocked himself out. As he fell his foot opened the tap on the gas copper releasing scalding water. Mother screamed when she spotted the water seeping under the bathroom door. Harry had to smash the bathroom window to get in and rescue Gus. The hole was later plugged with a rag and stayed that way for years. There's nothing like growing up with an unheated bathroom that has a cement floor and the wind whistling through a window, to make you appreciate today's comforts.

Two of my favorite lodgers were the brothers, Tom and Jerry. One brother would bang out a tune on our beat-up piano, while the other piped along on a penny whistle. No surprise these recitals happened after a long night at the pub.

"If you ever go across the sea to Ireland," began one of their favorites. I'll take you home again Kathleen," began another. I still love these mournful Irish songs.

The best looking lodger was Augustus Arthur with his coal black curls and mischievous light eyes. But he didn't stay long.

Through the window of the outside toilet, I overheard Mother talking to our neighbor, Mrs. Cook, over the privet hedge.

"He was arrested for carrying an iron pipe," I heard Mother say. I was hoping she wouldn't speak any lower or I wouldn't be able to hear who "he" was. "When Augustus went in front of the magistrate, he was asked why he was carrying an iron bar. 'Your Honor,'" Mother reported, imitating an even thicker Irish accent between bouts of laughter, "'there are some violent people on the streets, and you need to protect yourself.' The judge agreed and Augustus Arthur was sent packing back to Ireland," she told our neighbor.

I was reminded we had relatives in Ireland when the postman delivered parcels stamped "Eire" a few days before Saint Patrick's Day. Nestled between the butter and cheese would be sprigs of shamrock and miniature plastic harps. Mother would fashion a brooch and pin it to my jumper. I doubt there was a less Irish-looking kid in the whole school.

But if anyone asked, "Yes," I'd answer proudly, "my mother did come from Ireland."

****

"What Kept Ye?"

"Here's the list," Mother would say as she thrust the corner of an envelope and a shopping bag at me. "And don't break the eggs," she'd call after me. "And take the bike. It'll be quicker."

We had two bicycles. The boy's bike was the Old Man's transportation when our dad decided to go to work. The girl's bike, shared by eight kids, was black in the places it wasn't rusted and had no brakes. I had to reach up to grasp the handlebars and was either too little or too weak to push the pedals in a full circle.

We lived at the top of Mannock Road so I could gain some momentum before I needed to start my half-circle peddling. I never knew what clock my mother was watching when she decided that taking the bike made my trip to the shop quicker. I could have crawled faster.

Down Mannock Road I'd go taking a left by the red post box and on to Croyland Road and past the top gate of the infant school where I spent most of my time across the knee of Miss Swan, the headmistress. I'd take a right on Dale Street to Turnell's shop where I squeezed the brakes on the handlebars forgetting there were none—dragging my foot to bring the bike to a stop.

22

Mr. Turnell would reach down over the counter to take my shopping bag and the grocery list. He'd fill the bag with staples such as Heinz baked beans. Beans on toast would be our regular evening meal. He'd weigh the potatoes and the Brussel sprouts, cut, weigh, and wrap the cheese. In would go the green packet of loose leaf Brooke Bond tea, the packet of five Woodbine cigarettes, placing the six eggs on the top.

"Mum said she'll pay you next week," was my response to Mr. Turnell's outstretched hand.

"Your mum already owes me from last week."

I'd turn around and felt relief that there was nobody else in the shop.

Mr. Turnell would click his tongue, which I took as permission to leave. I'd grab the bag, haul it outside and hook it on the left handlebar. Back down Dale Street I'd wobble desperately trying to keep the bike upright as the filled grocery bag pulled me to one side. Lorries whizzed by me on Croyland Road. I dreaded making the turn onto Henshaw Road. While doing my slow half turns on the pedals, my left hand on the handlebar, and signaling with my right, my teeth would chatter as I made a frantic right turn across the intersection to the safety of the less-traveled Henshaw Road.

"What kept you?" my mother would ask as I stumbled, weak-kneed, into the kitchen, relieved to have cheated death once more. "What did Mr.

Turnell say?" my mother would inquire as she unpacked the grocery bag.

"He said we owed him from last week."

"I'll give him a couple of bob next week," she'd say matter-of-factly as she turned toward the gas stove to light up her Woodbine cigarette.

The town post office was just down the street from Turnell's grocery shop and occasionally Mother would make me go to the post office before school to cash the weekly family allowance coupon. The Government provided all families with cash assistance for each child, beginning with the second one. This weekly allowance was often the only money that kept a roof over our head and food on the table. The Old Man would call in sick if the weather was bad. And whatever money he had earned, he would blow at the pub on his way home on Friday nights.

No matter how much I whined about being late for school, Mother pushed me out of the back door and told me to "Get cracking and don't forget to pick me up a packet of cigs at the post office when you've cashed the coupon."

If the bike wasn't available I'd have to run to the post office, wait in a long line to cash the coupon and purchase Mother's cigarettes, then run home. I'd sprint to school, running the length of Croyland Park—over the bridge, up the hill, then down the streets of the Kingsway housing estate. Looming large was the keeper of the "late book" standing at the top of the school driveway.

I loathed being late for school. I was a good student, and a prefect—a position of authority reserved for well-behaved students. I proudly wore my shield-shaped prefect's badge on the lapel of my school uniform blazer.

I never knew if Mother cared how well I did at school. She wasn't the kind to give compliments. But one day, as I turned the corner at the side of our house, I overheard her talking over the privet hedge to our neighbor, Mrs. Cook.

"Our Pauline is doing ever so well in school," I heard her say. I must have smiled hearing the pride in her voice. But if there were a smile, it was wiped off pretty quickly when I heard her say, "Get the bike. The list is on the kitchen table."

****

Right and Left

October 19, 2016

If my mother had crossed the Atlantic Ocean to America instead of the Irish Sea to England, she would've been a fan of American politician, Bernie

Sanders. She'd have liked his mad hair and his passion.

As it was, London became her new home for a time. Had Mother stayed in the capital she might have favored another wild-haired politician—Boris Johnson.

Boris, you may know, is Britain's Secretary of State for Foreign and Commonwealth Affairs. Prior to this he served several terms as a member of Parliament, and before that as Mayor of London. He's a colorful character who amuses some and antagonizes others.

I first read about Boris in an online *Telegraph* article. Boris was Mayor when London hosted the 2012 Summer Olympics. Mayor Johnson, the newspaper reported, volunteered to be hoisted onto a 1,000-foot-long zip line as part of the Olympic celebrations. Trussed in a harness and sporting a blue hardhat while wildly waving a miniature Union Jack in each hand, he initially zoomed down the line before slowly rolling to a halt half-way along. As he dangled in mid-air the crowd, instead of rushing to his aid, pulled out their cell phone cameras. Boris smiled and waved his flags laughingly calling out, "Get me a ladder," as the crowd cheered. His aides eventually pulled him to safety.

A few years later when Boris was touted by others as a possible future Prime Minister, he responded, "How could anyone elect a prat who gets stuck on a zip wire?" It was an accurate prediction.

Had she delved deeper, Mother, I suspect, would have found Boris' antics funnier than his politics. When it came to Bernie Sanders, I have no doubt she would've joined her millennial great-grandson and cheered on the rebellion. Her anti-establishment politics were understandable. She'd spent her childhood among those yearning and fighting for Irish independence.

The British Labour Party, defenders of the working class, was the closest Mother could get to a political party that suited her personality. She'd sniff her disapproval of the Conservative Party. They were for the upper class—a bunch of out-of-touch snobs. Knowing how she felt, I was surprised when she fell in love with one.

Sidney was a short, balding, mustached Englishman. When he came to visit Mother, my seven siblings and I would squeeze onto the setee in the living room with the little ones sitting on the laps of the bigger kids. We'd be quiet for a change as we stared at this man. I was 12 years old then, old enough to wonder what man in his right mind would entangle himself with a woman who had eight children. Sid visited every evening. Mother tried to hide his shoes when he got ready to leave. One evening he stayed.

Although I couldn't understand Sid's attraction to our Mother—given all her baggage—it was easy to see why she fell for him. Sid was affectionate and attentive. The two kissed goodbye each morning—

unfamiliar behavior in our house. Sid startled me the first morning I passed him on the stairs as he brought Mother a cup of tea in bed. He did that every morning before he threw a leg over his bike and pedaled off to work.

Another time I laughed when I saw him teetering around the living room in his wool socks and my mother's high-heel shoes. Mother, who had swollen corns on her little toes, needed her new shoes stretched and Sid obliged.

After Sid moved in with us, the house seemed calmer and Mother laughed more often. But life wasn't perfect. As I mentioned, Sid voted Conservative.

One particular year Sid taped his Michael Hamilton Conservative Party flyer on the right side of the living room bay window. On the left window pane Mother posted her George Samuel Lingren Labour Party poster.

The curve of the bay window was Mother's favorite place to sit and peer from behind the white net curtains at passersby. Her cup of steaming Brooke Bond tea and smoldering Woodbine cigarette were permanent fixtures on the wide window ledge. She laughed as neighbors did double takes when they spied the political flyers. That year the Conservatives won. Sid may have had to cook his own dinner that election night. But I'd bet he took Mother her tea in bed the next morning.

****

Furry Friend or Foe

September 14 2017

My stepfather, Sid, loved ferrets. Like a lot of Englishmen, he used them to hunt wild rabbits, a menace to farmers' crops. Off Sid would trudge in his overcoat, wool cap, and knee-high Wellington boots. He'd slosh through soggy farm fields, along with a couple of mates, a 20-gauge shotgun in one hand and a sack carrying two wriggling ferrets in the other.

I thought about Sid's ferrets when I read an article recently about a group that was working to legalize ferret ownership in California.

"Is it just California that has ferrets on the no-pet list?" I asked my husband, Jim, hiding behind the sports page. He simply grunted.

"What's wrong with owning a ferret?" was my next question—apparently to myself since there was no movement from behind the newspaper in the recliner.

I knew Wikipedia would have the answer. If like me, you believe everything you read in the online encyclopedia, then ferrets are not only banned in California, but also in Hawaii, Washington D.C. and

New York City. These furry creatures are accused of carrying rabies, threatening agri-business, and are prone to biting owners and children. Poodles could check off two of those three, I thought.

I also learned there's at least one place in America that quite likes ferrets. "The Greatest Ferret Show on Earth" trumpets the website of the Greater Chicago Ferret Association. This event, now in its 29th year, claims to be the longest-running show of its kind in the United States. It is an event where proud owners parade their pets. Ferrets are judged for "colors, patterns, and structure based on the American Ferret Association preset standards." There's even a National Ferret Day—April 2nd. Who knew?

Apparently, British royalty is quite attached to the animal or was. If you happen to be loitering around Hatfield House in Hertfordshire—50 miles south of my hometown, where Queen Elizabeth I grew up in the mid sixteenth century—there's a portrait of Her Majesty hanging in the King James Drawing Room. She has what looks suspiciously like a ferret wearing a crown collar and clinging to the puffy sleeve of the Queen's jewel-studded black gown. The ferret is giving Good Queen Bess an adoring look.

I was a kid when Sid was into rabbit hunting. I only paid attention to the ferrets when he pulled them out of their cage in the back garden and stroked them before shoving them in a sack. Almost everyone in the family steered clear of the ferrets. We thought they were vicious little creatures ready to bite off a finger or two given a chance. The exception was Sid's son, Malcolm, who was born blind. A smile would cross his face when he felt the ferrets' fur. He couldn't see their sharp teeth.

One Saturday Sid returned from hunting minus one ferret. I overheard him tell a neighbor, "We lost a hob. We should have sent in a jill." The conversation made no sense to me. Sid explained that a hob and a jill are the names for the male and female ferret. "Usually," he said, "the ferret flushes out the rabbits for us, but sometimes they decide to have a snack while they're in the burrow and end up falling asleep. Hobs are more likely to do that than the jills. That's what happened last weekend. We couldn't get the blighter to come out."

Sid enjoyed his weekend hunts until he had what my mother called, "heart strains." Sid was in his sixties when he had an operation, courtesy of the National Health Service. Mother wrote that he was getting better, so I was stunned when she telephoned early one morning, and between choking sobs, told me Sid had a massive heart attack and died.

The suddenness of Sid's death was a shock, but the cause wasn't. He loved his beer and his dinner plates piled with mashed potatoes and meat, which often included the rabbits he caught. Mother would make curried rabbit, the spiciest dish I tasted as a child. Those familiar with English cooking will know what I mean.

Some weeks after Sid's death I was awakened by a phone call from Mother at two in the morning. She was probably having a cup of tea and a cigarette, watching the world go by through her bay window. I had been fast asleep in California.

Mother's voice was soft.

"I thought Sid would want me to scatter his ashes in the field where he liked to go rabbiting," she said. "Malcolm will go with me."

I cried, picturing my mother, arm-in-arm with Malcolm, fumbling their way through some cold, wet, weedy field, scattering the ashes of a beloved husband and father.

I'm glad Sid never knew that California has his adored ferrets on the no-pet list.

****

Many Happy Returns Mum

August 18, 2017

Had my mother lived, she would have been 100 years old in 2017.

I was 20 years old when I asked my mother for a copy of her birth certificate. It was part of the paperwork I needed to obtain my U.S. visa. She was not happy about my request; she was always secretive.

When the birth certificate arrived from Dublin, I discovered two things: the names of my grandparents, and my mother's date of birth.

I could never tell my mother how much it meant to me to read the names of her parents and to discover that my middle name was the same as my grandmother's first name. This might be a small thing to some, but for me the connection was a big thing. I never knew my father's name.

Under the birth certificate column, "Date and Place of Birth"—written in both English and Irish—I learned another fact. The date of my mother's birth was August 8, 1917. We'd always celebrated her birthday on the *ninth* of August. The dates were only one day apart, but the discovery felt like one more family mystery. My mother may have been surprised; she didn't say.

I think about my mum a lot, and not just on her birthday. I think about her every time I walk into my laundry room and see my washer and dryer. I remember how she had to kneel on a cement floor, her back bent over the bathtub, using a washboard to scrub clothes. A dry, windy day would bring a smile to Mother's face. It meant she wouldn't have to pull the washing off the backyard clothesline and string it up in the kitchen—turning the tiny room into a sauna.

When I watch films about World War II, I think about her. She gave birth to the first of her nine children under a bed in London during The Blitz— the relentless bombing by the Germans. Mother was eventually evacuated to the English countryside along with millions of other mothers, where I, and the rest of my siblings had the good fortune to be born and raised.

Coping with a houseful of squabbling kids, and living with a man who embodied every ugly stereotype ascribed to Irishmen, would be enough to drive anyone to drink. Fortunately for us kids Mother didn't hit the bottle, but she was a heavy smoker.

I slept in the room next to hers and I'd hear the click of the cigarette lighter before the sun rose.

She quit that terrible habit once. She telephoned me bright and early one morning, ignoring the time difference between England and California.

"I've stopped smoking," she said proudly. It lasted a week.

Nicotine helped calm her nerves she would tell me, and so apparently did caffeine. The whistling kettle was on the gas stove from morning 'till night. "Polly put the kettle on," Mother would say the minute I stepped into the kitchen.

Mother was not one to give compliments to anyone, least of all her kids. So it was a proud moment when she told me, "That's a lovely cup of tea." If I didn't wait long enough for the tea to brew, she was quick to complain that it tasted like urine—only she used a different word.

Gambling may have also helped her cope. The neighborhood bookie was Mr. Sharp, a short man with a flat cap who lived across the street. He'd zip through the garden gates and deliver the "Pink'Un," a horse racing tip sheet printed on pink paper. Mum would spread out the sports page from Saturday's newspaper, pick up a pin, close her eyes, and aim at the list of horses. She'd bet sixpence each way on the horse with the pin prick.

Mother eventually stopped betting on horses, but never lost her love of gambling. Bingo became her passion. When I telephoned her from America—in the days when it cost a small fortune—and it was a Bingo night, the call would be cut short. "Taxi is here. I'm going to Bingo."

In addition to smoking, drinking copious cups of tea, and gambling, add swearing to my mother's list of coping mechanisms.

Unlike the mothers of my English friends, my Irish mother swore constantly.

"Please don't swear, mum," I'd beg before my friends came to visit

She'd respond with a few swear words, but acted like a lady when they arrived.

For years, I rarely swore, an overreaction to the language that bounced off the walls of my childhood home.

Recently I read a *New York Times* article by Kristin Wong, which proclaimed that "researchers had concluded that swearing had the effect of reducing sensitivity to pain." Mother was self-medicating and didn't know it. Had I known swearing was therapeutic I would have started much earlier.

It's a strange thing to admit, but I think my mum would have liked that.

1585 "Ermine" portrait of Queen Elizabeth I
by Nicholas Hilliard

THE ROYALS

My mother was no fan of British Royalty. If you know anything about Irish history you'll understand why. Unlike my mother, I enjoyed hearing about the Royal Family. Queen Elizabeth II was a princess when I was a child. I'd flip through glossy magazine photographs of Elizabeth and her sister Margaret. They lived in a magical world—gliding around in shimmering ball gowns and sparkling tiaras. Horse-

drawn coaches carted them from one palace to another. I'd drift away to this fairy-tale land as I toasted my toes by the coal fire. The following columns *"A King, A Queen, and a Coronation,"* shares my memories of some historic occasions. *"Three Degrees of Separation" and "Downton's Done"* pokes gentle fun at some British traditions and the aristocracy.

A King, a Queen, and a Coronation

January 6, 2017

My ears prick up when Britain's royalty is mentioned. I grew up over there watching grainy newsreels of Queen Elizabeth II and her two young children, Charles and Anne, frolicking with at least ten Welsh Corgis. Balmoral Castle—their 50,000-acre Scottish estate—loomed in the background.

I was carried away again recently when glued to the television watching *The Crown*—a drama chronicling the Queen's early reign. I felt myself growing older by the minute—surprised by how much of this history I'd shared.

I was seven years old when on a damp February evening in 1952, my older sister, Sheila, and I walked arm-in-arm toward her friend Barbara's house. We were reciting poetry out loud as we often did. That night it was Sheila's favorite poem, Daffodils, by William Wordsworth. "I wander lonely as a cloud ...." we began in unison.

Our voices echoed in the eerie silence. We'd soon learn why the gas-lit streets were quiet. The BBC had cancelled all broadcasts. Our 57-year-old King George had died. The following year our town, like every other in Britain, was consumed with preparing for the coronation of Elizabeth, the King's 25-year-old daughter. Colorful streamers, and Union Jacks of all sizes, stretched across narrow streets and hung from rooftops. Coronation committees were formed—parades were planned, bonfires and fireworks would be lit on village greens, and church bells would ring out across the land.

On Coronation Day, tables and chairs were hauled out of brick row houses and lined up in the road ready for street parties. I sat shoulder to shoulder with the rest of the neighborhood kids and wolfed down cake and ice cream. The coronation mug and spoon the council gave to each child is long gone. Nothing lasted in our house.

I have the Queen's uncle, Edward VIII, to thank for the cake and ice cream. Edward's abdication led to the crowning of his younger brother George—the Queen's father—which made Elizabeth heir to the throne. I was reminded while watching *The Crown* how mesmerized the world was by all this royal drama.

Although the abdication happened before my time—80 years ago to be exact—I learned all about it, and never forgot how important it was. Edward's cavalier attitude towards duty to country has been contrasted with that of the Queen's. Some say she will never abdicate—that she'll honor the oath she made to govern the rest of her life.

It looks like the Queen will keep that promise. She's 90 years old and has reigned for 64 years. Winston Churchill was her first prime minister. Across the pond, Harry S. Truman was President. Elizabeth has seen 13 Prime Ministers and 11 Presidents, come and go. There are two presidents she has reason to remember—both named Bush.

When visiting George H. W. Bush at the White House, the Queen, who is 5' 4", was led to a podium that was so high, only her hat was visible. Her speech was labelled "the talking hat." I can hear the collective gasp from the Brits.

Fast forward 16 years and another Bush is President. Famous for his gaffs, "W" did not disappoint. When referring to a visit the Queen had made decades earlier, George W. praised the monarch saying, "You helped our nation celebrate its bicentennial in 177—uh, in 1976"—quickly correcting his aging of Her Majesty by 200 years. The President then *winked* at the Queen of England.

I can't imagine travelling as much as the Queen still does. Who could blame her if she did step down? A few years ago the Netherland's 75-year-old

Queen Beatrix handed the crown to her son, Prince Willem-Alexander.

The British throne has been elusive to Queen Elizabeth's 68-year-old heir, Prince Charles. I remember a political cartoon in which Charles shows his mother the article about the abdication of Queen Beatrix. The caption read: "Have you seen this, mummy?"

At times, I have been referred to as 'the queen.' It stems, I'm told, from my habit of raising my nose before saying something self-righteous. To cement this perception I was given a gift of a two-inch square alabaster fridge magnet. Below the embossed crown are the words, "Don't treat me any differently than you would the Queen."

In response, I offer these words (nose raised)— spoken by the Queen in *The Crown*: "... for better or worse, the crown has landed on my head."

****

Three Degrees of Separation

April 22, 2016

As the world celebrates the 90th birthday of the Queen of England, I think it's a perfect time to brag about my connection to Her Majesty. I was made aware of this relationship via a message from London.

My friend Della began her email to me with a surprising announcement. Her younger sister—a former member of the British Parliament—had been appointed to the House of Lords and honored with the title of baroness. Della informed me that from now on her sister would be referred to as Lady something.

"Curtsey practice happening now," Della signed off. I was impressed.

I grew up in a working class country town northeast of London and the only times I heard the title of "Lady" used was when my sister, Doris, whose mission in life was to reduce me to tears once a day, referred to me as " Lady Muck."

In preparation for the unlikely event that I'd meet the baroness, I decided to brush up on the workings of the British Government. I'd forgotten most of what I learned in school. In my mid-teens (at an age when I might have retained something), I was busy backcombing my hair and desperately searching for a boyfriend. I did remember some general details: the Prime Minister is head of the government. There are two houses of Parliament: The House of Commons, whose members are elected, and a House of Lords, whose seats are either appointed or inherited.

The House of Lords, where Della's sister will be seated, is frequent fodder for the British press, which scream for reform. After reading there are almost 800 members of this House, I understood why. A curious fact is there are only 400 physical seats for this crowd, which means if everyone shows up, one-half would end up sitting on someone's lap.

The annual Opening of Parliament occurs in May. It's a formal affair, presided over by the Queen as Head of State. Like many British traditions, this event includes ceremonies simultaneously regal and perplexing. Prior to the Queen's arrival at the Opening, the Yeomen of the Guard search the cellars. This practice began in 1605 when Guy Fawkes, a Catholic rebel, was discovered in the basement with 36 barrels of gunpowder and no plausible explanation. He planned to blow up the place and assassinate the reigning Protestant King James I, thereby restoring the monarchy to the Catholics. Known thereafter as "The Gunpowder Plot," this thwarted act of treason is memorialized as Guy Fawkes Day on November 5th throughout Great Britain.

As a child I joined with other kids in this "celebration" by hauling around a scarecrow-like figure stuffed with newspapers. A cardboard sign strung around its neck begged for a "Penny for the Guy" that we would use to buy fireworks that lit up the evening sky. The "Guys" went up in flames perched on backyard bonfires. Years later it dawned on me I had been celebrating a macabre tradition, which, I admit, did not interfere one bit with my enjoyment.

A parliamentary tradition which falls under the "perplexing" column is the holding of a hostage. While the Queen is at the Houses of Parliament, a member of Parliament is held "hostage" at Buckingham Palace to guarantee her safe return. It might just be me, but somehow it doesn't appear to be exactly an even swap should the monarch not be allowed to return to the palace.

Suitably crowned and robed, The Queen takes a seat on her throne in the House of Lords. Before she begins her speech, she dispatches the Black Rod to invite the 250 elected representative of the House of Commons to join the gathering. As a person of color, I admit that when I first saw the words, "Black Rod," I had the sinking feeling that a Black man, representing a symbol of a bygone Empire, would be the messenger.

Black Rod, it turns out, is just that, a black rod—a three-foot long ebony rod carried by a messenger dressed in black.

At the next opening of Parliament, the baroness, sister of my friend Della, will be there within curtsying distance of the Queen of England.

How's that for three degrees of separation?

****

Downton's Done

March 21, 2016 The Union

I didn't visit my mother in England as often as I should. The goodbyes were too painful. Each one I thought would be the last, and then one was.

Most people look forward to retirement, but I dreaded saying goodbye to my co-workers. I knew my stiff upper lip wouldn't hold up. The timed lights in my government office shut off one evening as I stayed late to clear off my desk so I could skip going in the next morning—my retirement day. I delayed my retirement party until I could compose myself.

Now here I am saying goodbye again. This time it isn't to anyone I loved or enjoyed working with. In fact these people aren't even real. They are the cast of a British public television series *Downton Abbey*. I was preparing to watch the final two-hour episode.

For readers who wouldn't be caught dead watching public television, here's a synopsis of the series: Lord and Lady Grantham and their three daughters—the Crawley family, plus a cellar full of servants, occupy Downton Abbey, a sprawling grey manor in North Yorkshire. The Crawley clan spends their days sipping tea, their nights swilling cocktails, and is seemingly incapable of putting on, or taking off, their own clothes without the help of a lady's maid, or a valet.

Out of respect for the series' finale, I wore a crimson wool hat, a gift from my friend, Jeane, who said it looked like something out of *Downton Abbey*, and would look great on me. I agreed with her first assertion, but disputed the second. Any hat I've ever worn added at least ten years. On the side table in my living room, next to the settee, I placed a box of ultra-soft Kleenex, and a Royal Stuart bone china cup and saucer retrieved from the china cabinet. I was ready to say farewell.

Over the span of the series I've fancied myself as Lady Mary, the beautiful and clever daughter of Lord Grantham, the Crawley patriarch. I gradually went off her, though, as her tongue became sharp enough to cut a hedge, as my Irish cousin Mick would say. I transferred my allegiance to the raven-haired, rebellious Lady Sybil, Mary's sister, who flaunted social conventions by marrying Tom Branson, who was not only a chauffeur, but an Irish one at that.

Tom loved Lady Sybil, but hated the English aristocracy with their history of Irish repression. Tom reminded me of the assortment of curly-headed lodgers my Irish stepfather brought home from the pub, fresh off their voyage from Ireland to England. Lubricated with more than a few pints of Guinness, they'd bang out a tune on our dilapidated piano as they sang their mournful ballads, yearning for the land they left.

Back to Downton. Forever bustling about in the servants' kitchen would be Mrs. Patmore, the pleasant and plump cook. She reminded me of another cook from my childhood, our neighbor, Mrs. Cook. As I watched Mrs. Patmore, I could see Mrs. Cook waddling down her garden path to the privet hedge that separated her backyard. Puffs of flour would rise as she dusted off hands interrupted while baking. She was responding to a "Yoo hoo, Mrs. Cook," from my mother, similarly clad in a wrap-around pinafore dress. Mother may have been calling to borrow a cup of sugar that would never be repaid or perhaps she needed a counselling session.

The final episode of Downton Abbey tidies up nicely. There was the wedding that nobody thought would happen. I was waiting for the bride's dead ex-fiancé to materialize after the words, "speak now or forever hold your peace." He didn't. There was the maid who gave birth to her baby in Milady's bed, and all three survived this breach of protocol. The conniving footman sought and found redemption, and Lady Mary retracted her switchblade.

Reviews throughout the series confirmed that everyone's favorite character was Lord Grantham's "Mama"—The Dowager Countess, played to perfection by Maggie Smith. Her pithy one-liners became legendary. My favorite, and one I relate to as a retired person, was when she innocently asks someone, "What's a weekend?"

During the final episode the Dowager bowed out with yet another memorable quip about her just-married niece, Lady Edith.

"With any luck, they'll be happy enough, which is the English version of a happy ending."

The Union Jack and the Star Spangled Banner
flying over the London Bridge relocated from
London to Lake Havasu City, Nevada

BLOKES AND YANKS

*The piece: "**The Reunion**," is dedicated to the American airmen who were barely out of their teens when stationed at RAF Bentwaters, England 50 years ago. These young Americans called all English people "Blokes," and the English called all Americans, "Yanks."*

Although the British and American language is collectively called "English," both nationalities spell, pronounce, and use words that confound the other. These confusions are treated with humor, or should I *say humour, as I have in "**You say Tomayto...,**" and "**Snogging and the Trade Deficit.**"*

The Reunion

May 31, 2018

Spending five days with eleven ex-servicemen in a hotel in Laughlin, Nevada did not sound appealing to me. The trip became more inviting, however, when I learned that Sharron and Pat, two women who I had enjoyed meeting in years past, were also going to be there.

The occasion was the 50-year reunion of my husband's Air Force buddies. Most of the guys were barely out of their teens when they were whisked away from the U.S. in the late 1960s, and spent three years in England at an East Anglian Air Base by the North Sea.

Jim had stayed in touch with several of these old friends: the three Davids traveling from Florida, Kentucky, and Washington state, and Ed from Indiana. Others attending were Larry and Joe from Texas, Richard from Georgia, Denny from Missouri, Gary from Utah, and the reunion instigator, Mike from Iowa.

Relaxing in our hotel room, I asked Jim what he remembered about his friends. He told me that Ed and Washington Dave was always joking, while Kentucky Dave was the responsible one. "He was always the designated driver."

Jim didn't hang out with Richard from Georgia but remembered he wore a three-piece suit and had at least three girls hanging on his arm. When I met Richard, I saw he still had a woman on his arm—an attractive blond wife who, shall we say, looked slightly younger than the rest of us wives.

During one of our dinners, I sat next to Larry's wife Lynn, a retired school teacher. I was surprised and impressed to learn that Larry had pursued a singing career. Since they live in Texas I assumed country music. Wrong. He's an opera singer, a tenor soloist who has performed internationally. Joe, the other Texan, handed out business cards which proudly advertised his metal artworks. Very cool, I thought.

Two of the couples had been married when they lived in England. There were Gary and Carol from Utah. "Nobody remembers me," Gary said more than once. Apparently, he was too busy being married to hang out with the guys at the Airmen's Club.

Florida Dave and Pat were the other young couple. Dave, with the approval of his current wife, had invited ex-wife Pat and Lisa, their adult daughter. Lisa had been born in England and Jim stayed at the hospital with Dave while Pat gave birth.

"I was only 20 years old when Pat had the baby," Jim said giving Lisa a fatherly look across the table one morning in the hotel restaurant. "We all felt like she was our kid too."

There was no shortage of entertainment. We sang. We danced. Some performed Karaoke. Mike and Denny, the singing guitarists, serenaded us under the poolside cabana along with Debbie, Richard's wife. As expected there was an ample supply of alcohol but nobody got drunk—surprising since two mason jars labeled "moonshine" and "white lightning" occasionally appeared.

Mike, the reunion organizer, chose Laughlin because of its proximity to Lake Havasu and the London Bridge. Several of the guys had visited the bridge in London while it was being dismantled in 1968, the year the bridge was auctioned off to the American oilman and chainsaw magnate, Robert P. McCullough, for $2,460,000.

McCullough purchased the bridge for his dream city in the desert—26 square miles of barren, desolate land he'd purchased for $73.47 acre. It is the only bridge ever erected on dry land. A mile-long channel was later dredged to capture the water that now flows under the bridge from the main body of Lake Havasu. The reassembled bridge was dedicated on October 10, 1971.

I was living in England when the bridge was sold. I thought how sad it was that England was selling an iconic landmark to someone who was going to stick it in the middle of the Arizona desert. One London headline blared, "London Bridge Falls to the Apaches," an inaccurate reference to Havasu which in fact, means "blue water" in the Mojave Indian language. The reality was the 130-year-old bridge was sinking under the weight of ever-increasing London traffic. The local council had planned to tear it down and replace it, but McCullough preserved the landmark.

Jim and his friends lined up for group photographs on the bridge, beside the bridge, and crammed into an iconic British red phone box. We ate fish and chips scooped into fake newsprint and drowned in vinegar. The Brit's favorite food tasted almost as good as what is served at Auburn's Pelican's Roost, a restaurant my English-born friend, Bill, who lives in Lake Wildwood, frequents.

New memories were made and friendships rekindled all thanks to Mike and Mel, our gracious hosts. We have pledged to meet again in two years. It sounds appealing.

****

You Say "Tomayto and I say Tomahto"

April 6, 2015, The Union

This is an open letter to Nigel Thrift, vice chancellor and president of the University of Warwick in England. Mr. Thrift was in Placer County recently to provide details on a proposed 6,000-student Warwick University to be built on 600 acres west of Roseville. I hope he's still in the area so he can read this.

Dear Vice Chancellor/President Thrift:

May I say your surname is perfect for someone looking for investors for the new University of Warwick proposed for construction in Placer County. Also, your Christian name, or should I say "first name", is pretty cool too—very upper-class English. How many Americans are named Nigel?

This letter has nothing whatsoever to do with your nice name, but more to do with the difference between English and American pronunciation. I was born and raised about 50 miles east of Coventry where your Warwick University is located. I know it's not news to you, or to most Brits and Americans, that though we mostly understand each other's language—facilitated by American films in Great Britain, and British programs on American public television, there are still some words and pronunciations that cause confusion.

In my teens I dated an American serviceman who was stationed in England. He would become my first, but not my last husband.

"Frank the Yank," as my cheeky siblings called him, was a bit odd. Even I, a self-centered teenager at the time, managed to discern his quirkiness. I continued to date him. I told myself Frank's behavior was just a cultural thing, something to be understood—like his Southern accent. One of his many quirks was to correct my pronunciation.

"Nestlés chocolate is American," he announced one rainy afternoon as he sat on our sofa in the living room munching a chocolate Aero bar, "and it's pronounced "Neslees" not "Nessels.""

He also said I pronounced "aluminium" incorrectly. "It's not al-you-min-i-um," he told me mockingly. "It's a-loo-min-um."

As I'm sure you've experienced during your illustrious career, this English versus American pronunciation is typically dealt with in a lighthearted manner—providing fodder for fun between the two nationalities. You've probably heard about the American serviceman whose smile disappeared when he found out that his British girlfriend's request to "knock me up in the morning," referred to a wake-up knock on her door. I hope I'm not being too familiar.

I don't know if you're renting a car while you're visiting Placer County, but if you are, know that Americans have a different word for the hinged cover over the engine. They call it "the hood." If you travel to Amish country and have car trouble, asking a mechanic "to look under the bonnet," might get you more than a suspicious look.

My current husband once told me how he learned the name of another British car part.

He and a couple of other American servicemen stationed in England were walking towards the Running Buck, a huge bar in the town of Ipswich in East Anglia, a few miles from their assigned airbase. The English bartender and avid hunter, affectionately known as Dickie Bird, was walking with them.

"I have to remember I have a bunny in my boot," Dickie Bird said—thinking out loud.

My husband responded with, "A bunny in your boot? You can't have a bunny in your boot."

"I bet you five pounds I do," Dickie Bird replied.

"You're on," said my husband.

"Follow me," said Dickie Bird, and led the group back to the car park. Dickie Bird lifted the lid on the trunk of his car, and there, on the pages of the *News of the World*, lay a dead rabbit.

"There's the bunny in the boot," said Dickie Bird, and he held out his hand.

Getting back to the University of Warwick.

I suggest that when the time comes to develop an entrance exam for the new college, that you give priority to the following pass/fail oral test. Before any of the projected 6,000 students set foot on the campus of the University of Warwick, Roseville, they must correctly pronounce "The University of

Warwick." I have no doubt that 100 percent of those applying for college entry will be able to pronounce the first three words: "The University of." It's the fourth word, "Warwick," that will trip them up.

I've heard Warwick pronounced by local television newscasters as "Worwick" and "Warewick."

The correct pronunciation, as you and I know, is Wha (as in "what") rick—Warick. I would be willing to sit on the oral examination board.

There's one mispronunciation that manages to make me laugh out loud no matter how often I hear it.

After 40-plus years of marriage, and numerous elocution lessons, my husband still manages to mispronounce Worcestershire, as in Worcestershire sauce. He pronounces it phonetically, "Woor-cest-er-shire." The correct pronunciation, as you and I know, is the British way—"Woo-ster-sheer."

Since I am correcting him, and he is not correcting me, I think my current husband will be my last one.

With the utmost sincerity,

Postscript: Unfortunately, the University of Warwick canceled its plans to build the campus in Placer County. I hope it wasn't anything I said.

****

Snogging and the Trade Deficit

June 1, 2017

I hadn't seen or heard the word "snogging," since I was a teenager in the East Midlands where I spent more than one evening with a boy, doing just that, in the red phone box on the corner of Henshaw and Mannock Roads. So I was surprised to see the word in Tricia Caspers' *Auburn Journal* column, "How to Survive a Heartbreak?"

I asked my husband if snogging was also an American word. "Nope," he said.

I asked my American daughter-in-law if she knew what snogging was.

"Yes," she said. "I read it in Harry Potter."

So, I shouldn't have been surprised that an American was using a British word. Lately the trans-Atlantic language trade has begun to even out. There was a time when Britain operated under a huge deficit. America was flooding the market. I blame those good-looking U.S. servicemen stationed in Britain, dazzling us all with their American twang. When was the last time a British soldier was billeted in America? Not since the 1800s, I'd guess. And then there were the American films.

My friends and I would be glued to the Lyric Cinema screen soaking up every word that drawled from the Yankee lips of Clark Gable, Marlon Brando and Gary Cooper. How many British film stars from the 50s and 60s could an American name? We watched English films, too. But before the explosion of the "New Wave"—films that focused on the British working class—all the English actors used a cigarette holder, had posh accents and repressed emotions. In the American films, cigarettes dangled daringly from lips, and, unlike the English, you couldn't tell who had money by the way they spoke.

Since American words and phrases are not required to be identified as "made in America," young Brits have no idea their language has been Americanized. Nobody said, "Hi" or "Bye," when I was growing up. In my country town we greeted each other with, " 'ello me duck," or 'ow are yu." Our goodbyes were "Cheerio, love" or "Tudah."

I've read that "awesome" has become a popular word in Britain. Apparently it has taken the place of "marvelous," a wonderfully upper-class English word, usually followed by "darling." I've yet to hear any Brit call a loved one "honey," but that can't be far off. Compare "awesome, honey," with "marvelous, darling." I know which I prefer.

Another word that has sprung up over the pond is "prom." They even have proms. Not too long ago these milestone events were non-existent in British schools. Dance parties were called discos, or my preferred term: "balls."

Seeing "snogging" in print was a surprise that brought back fond memories. But there are some British words and phrases that should never have left "that green and pleasant land." How did that awful "gobsmacked" pass customs? My Irish mother often threatened to "smack my gob," but "gobsmacked" as one word—meaning shocked—I'd never heard until recently. I could imagine Paul McCartney using the word so I blame the Liverpudlians, who are mostly Irish anyway. And while I'm complaining, what's with this "one off"— another ghastly British phrase Americans have adopted? Notice the word, "ghastly." I think Prince Charles is the only one licensed to use that adjective.

Back to those U.S. servicemen in England. It wasn't only their accents that were attractive to the locals. They were just so casual. They wore jackets, called windbreakers, which zipped up and ended at their waists. Our boys were wearing thigh-length jackets with velvet collars and calling themselves Teddy Boys—emulating the Edwardian era.

The Americans wore buttoned-down shirts. They chewed gum. They smoked Lucky Strikes and still had white teeth. My teenage friends and I scooted up close to these boys when queuing up for the green double-decker bus. The soldiers were always laughing. And why wouldn't they? They were young, single, away from their parents, and making more money than any of the local lads. It's no wonder snogging was on the rise.

ॐॐ

George's Watercolor

COMING TO AMERICA

When I told my mother I was moving to California—leaving the English seaside town of Felixstowe with my two young children—she said I was mad (as in nuts). She must have forgotten she was talking to her strong-willed daughter.

*"**First California Christmas**" is a sweet memory of my first Christmas with Jim, the man I left home for. "**Summer of Love**" tells when the music of the Beatles on a hot California summer evening took me back to when Jim and I first met. The idea for the "**Crackers Anyone?**" column occurred when a young*

clerk in a retail shop replied: *"We don't sell food here"* when I asked if they sold Xmas crackers. A painting on my wall inspired *"**Allergy Season**"* and reinforced that it's the people I remember, not the work. *"'**Till Death Us Do Part**" is a tribute to my in-laws. I wrote *"**I Can See Clearly Now**"* to remind myself I'm older than I think, and *"**Discoveries**"* so a special connection would never be forgotten.*

First California Christmas

December 15, 2016

Mother had taken the train—something she rarely did. Her kids visited her, not the other way around. We sat in my upstairs flat by the bay window—Mother puffing on her Senior Services cigarette as I stared out at the grey North Sea.

"You're mad," she'd said earlier. "Dragging these kids halfway around the world." She meant to say, "Don't go. I'll miss you."

It was December 1970, and I was a week away from leaving Felixstowe, a seaside town in East Anglia, to move to California. I'd fallen in love with an American airman.

My mother wasn't the only one who thought I'd lost my mind.

America is such a violent country," one worried friend reminded me between bites of a sausage roll at my work going-away party. "They assassinated their President, *and* Martin Luther King, *and* Bobby Kennedy."

I wasn't worried. I'd lived a year in New Mexico and Texas, and had managed to survive. Besides, I wasn't moving to America. I was moving to California.

Thanks to Georgia, my American friend, and her "Get Pauline to America" fund drive, enough money was raised to fly me and the children to New York, but not enough to fly to California. Getting to Sacramento would take three long days on buses decorated with a galloping racing dog.

Jim, the man I'd left home for, met us at the Greyhound bus station on L Street in downtown Sacramento. He was driving a fire-engine red Chevelle Super Sport. Jim had purchased the car four months before being drafted and whisked off to England for three years. There were times, his mother had told him, when she was driving the Chevy and teenage guys in muscle cars would pull up beside her, flash her a grin, and rev their engines. She admitted to being tempted.

With Jim driving, and the children and I settled into the black tuck and roll seats, the Chevy easily climbed the winding Highway 50. Jim grew up camping in the Sierra Nevada and was excited to show us Hope Valley, one of the lush high-mountain meadows where his family pitched their tents and fished for Rainbow Trout in the snow-melt streams.

"This brings back memories," Jim said as he deftly shifted into third gear. "My dad had a Volkswagen Bug. The car was packed to the headliner with our camping gear. Mom was in the front and my two brothers and I were in the back. This was the 50s before Highway 50 was built and we took two-lane roads from downtown Sacramento to the mountains. Since my brother, Ray, and I were the two oldest kids, when we reached the steepest hill, my dad would tell us to jump out of the car to lighten the load. We'd race each other up the hill ahead of the sputtering Bug. Our baby brother, Mike, lounged in the back seat grinning like a Cheshire cat."

On our return trip Jim pulled into a turnout. As the children and I jabbered about what we'd seen that day, Jim wandered off. When he returned he answered the question asked by my raised eyebrows. It's a broken branch, he'd said. We had our Christmas tree.

Back in the apartment Jim nailed the branch to a small wooden cross he'd made as a support, and centered it on the vinyl tabletop. Soon our cramped second-story apartment was filled with popping sounds, and the toasty smell of popcorn.

Jim demonstrated how to string the puffy kernels together with a needle and thread, and wound the string around the tree—a holiday decoration new to me and the kids. He was kept busy trying to pop enough corn to replace what the kids kept eating.

I stepped back from the table to admire the decorated tree. Jim said it needed something. He tore the flap off a cardboard box and cut it into the shape of a star. He showed the kids how to cover it with aluminum foil, and then tied it to the top of the tree.

I knew I'd taken a chance "dragging the kids halfway across the world," as my mother had said.

But Jim had already shown he was as caring as I'd hoped. I knew everything would be all right.

****

Crackers Anyone?

January 3, 2016

My American family indulged me yet again. They agreed to pull Christmas crackers, a cylindrical foil popper that makes a cracking sound when tugged apart, and sit through dinner wearing a paper crown that periodically slips from the head into the turkey gravy. The crown, along with a written joke, a trivia question and a totally useless trinket, are encased in the cracker and the reward for each guest who participates.

Placing crackers on the Christmas dinner table is one of the few British traditions that I keep alive.

There's no Christmas pudding—a fruit cake doused in brandy. No Christmas cake, an even fruitier cake, covered with a layer of marzipan topped with hard icing and decorated with Christmas figurines. I've totally let the British ex-pat side down. I was reminded of this while watching the British television series, Indian Summers, set in the 1930s. The English ruling class living in India during those glorious Empire days did a much better job than I do of inflicting their superior culture on the natives. English roses bloomed in deserts and hot tea was served daily under the scorching Indian sun.

My English women friends, who, like me, have lived in California for decades, are better cultural ambassadors than I. They drink Typhoo tea, eat Cadbury's chocolates, and munch on McVities Digestive Biscuits. Up to a few years ago, they paid exorbitant prices at English specialty shops for these treats.

Now most grocery stores have a small section dedicated to these imports. I had to look twice during a visit to my local supermarket when I spotted the hated Tate and Lyle's Golden Treacle on the shelf. The green and gold tin brought back memories of my English school dinners. This sickly syrup was poured over a grey mound in an effort to add flavor to something with the appropriately nondescript name of "steam pudding."

It's not only British traditions that I've let go by the wayside. I've lost most of my accent, although some people have accused me of being Australian. I've also been asked if I'm Jamaican. I attribute this to my brown skin and curly black hair. Most Americans haven't adapted to the fact that not all British people are a shade whiter than pale.

My English friends, though, sound like they just got off the boat. They are military wives, clustered around an air force base where they hear and speak British English.

One of my first jobs in California was working in a typing pool. I was required to learn "American" so my co-workers could understand me when we proof-read letters. These young women translated my "full stop" to "period," my "inverted commas" to "quotation marks," and my "brackets" to "parentheses." I'm not sure they'd have been able to translate my English friends' "aye up, wonky, or having a dekko." You may have to look these up.

I'm not a total loss, though. I make sausage rolls—small savory snacks of sausage meat encased in puff pastry. I've been complimented on my fish and chips and I make a dash to Grass Valley every few months to pick up Cornish pasties that my American husband mispronounces—apparently confusing them with women's undergarments. I drink Typhoo tea when my English friends visit, use a teapot and put the milk in the cup before pouring the tea.

On the subject of beverages I'm reminded of the stop at my ex-husband's mother's house in Roanoke, Virginia during my first visit to America.

"Would you like some tea," she asked in her lilting Southern accent. The irony of the scene—the middle-aged white southern woman waiting on the young brown-skinned girl—didn't occur to me until decades later.

"Yes, please," was my reply. I was dying for a cuppa. Minutes later my mother-in-law handed me a tall glass with ice cubes bobbing in brown liquid. I took a polite sip and hoped my forced smile disguised my utter distaste for this concoction that I'd learn later was called "iced tea." I couldn't wait to write home to my mother. Cold tea is the worst thing you can offer a guest in England.

****

Summer of Love

August 9, 2017

Any song performed by the four Liverpool lads takes me back to a quiet seaside town on the east coast of England. My rented upstairs flat was a bit dingy even after I painted the kitchen walls orange, but I could see the roiling North Sea through the bay window.

My then boyfriend, Jim, an American airman, would sit with me on the threadbare carpet and listen to Radio Luxembourg, one of the few stations that played popular music. The Beatles' songs were our favorites. The line that included "...let her into your heart..." from the song "Hey Jude" would make us both misty-eyed knowing when Jim's three-year tour ended that we might never see each other again.

Jim returned to America and kept his promise that he would write. One year later boyfriend Jim, became husband Jim.

Decades later, Jim unfolds my red lawn chair on the grassy slope of an open air amphitheater in the California foothills. We're there to hear *Mania*, a Beatles tribute band. One of the first songs they sang was "Hey Jude,"—our song." I didn't care that they sang with fake Liverpudlian accents and discernable American twangs.

The music was great, but the temperature had soared to triple digits that day and was still uncomfortable at six in the evening. At least the audience was in the shade. I felt sorry for the performers though, the sun beat directly onto the stage.

I rarely complain about California weather. If I start, images from my childhood in England kick in. I see myself jumping out of bed and racing to the bedroom window. If it wasn't raining, it was a good day. Even when it was dry in the morning the weather forecasters' "chances of rain," constantly hovered over the island. Perspective is a wonderful thing.

In contrast to those gloomy bygone days, the scene at the *Mania* show would have inspired a Norman Rockwell painting. Throngs of picnickers sat cross-legged on blankets or lounged in low-back lawn chairs, eating and drinking and filling the sultry air with chatter and laughter. Children chased each other around the few open areas. Everyone was well-behaved, with one exception. A frisky Jack Russell Terrier had escaped its leash and was dancing on two legs with a little boy. The pair was spinning in circles in the emergency walkway.

I had learned about the summer concert from my hiking friend, Hazel, a retired teacher, who knows a lot about a lot, especially the plants we encounter during our early morning group hikes. Hazel doesn't know this, but a memory she shared was one of the sweetest I've ever heard. She told me a young pupil once said: "Miss taught me how to laugh."

I soaked in the evening: listening, remembering and watching the antics of the Sugar Plump Fairies. Yes, "plump" is how these ladies, who dress in dazzling costumes, describe themselves. They frolic about doing "fun raising" for charitable events, collecting donations. On this evening, the donations they collected benefitted Placer Arts, a non-profit that has hosted 29 years of free summer concert series.

During the Beatles' show, a fairy in her tie-dye hippie costume, replete with flowers in her hair, floated down the aisle where I was sitting. She extended her hand and hoisted me from my lawn chair. As I was plucked from my seat, I peered over my shoulder and mouthed "help" to my hiking friends. They were too busy laughing to come to my rescue. My husband looked the other way.

Hand-in-hand down the grassy slope we went toward a dance area near the stage.

It was 1968 when the Beatles' "Hey Jude" single was released—two years before Jim left England to go home. On our last night together I'd cooked him a roast leg of lamb in the tiny kitchen of my seaside flat. I wanted to impress Jim. He'd told me how much he enjoyed the lamb meals his Basque grandfather had often prepared.

I almost didn't make it back to the States," Jim wrote to me later.

He'd left my place so late he didn't know if he'd get back to the base in time to sign his exit papers. A lorry driver had picked him up and drove Jim right to the base gate after hearing his story.

"The window blinds at the sign-out office were pulled down, and the door was locked," he told me. Jim banged on the locked door. No answer. He kept banging. An eye peered between one of the horizontal slats. The door opened.

"Hey, dude," the airman scowled—annoyed he had to open up the office.

Not exactly "Hey, Jude," but close enough to remind Jim of our favorite song.

****

Allergy Season

June 25, 2017

There are gifts and then there are gifts.

I giggled when I first heard the name George Winkleblack, but managed to keep a straight face when I found out he had become my boss.

I could see George out of the corner of my eye as I sat at my grey metal desk in a government office with grey walls and grey vinyl floor tiles.

Mr. Winkleblack looked a lot like Jimmy Stewart—long-legged and rangy. He didn't stand; he leaned—sometimes against the door frame of his corner office. He didn't sit, he reclined—feet on his oak desk, legs crossed at the ankles.

George was not a big talker so I was surprised that Monday morning when he took two long strides out of his office and sat on the corner of my desk. He stared out of the window. He'd visited his wife's grave over the weekend, he told me. I'd heard George was a widower, married for decades. After kneeling to put flowers in front of his wife's gravestone he found it difficult to stand. He'd never had trouble like that before. His doctor told him it was grief.

The Mobile Equipment Office that George managed was on the ground floor of a high rise in downtown Sacramento. I'd fumbled my way through the State government's hiring maze, and landed a job after flashing my business college credentials and barely passing the typist test at 45 words per minute.

At least I could touch type. Before I emigrated from England, I'd faked typing skills to get a job and ended up getting the sack. Hunt and peck didn't get it when a shoe factory came to a standstill waiting for my work orders. This humiliating episode drove me to attend a business college as soon as my stilettos hit American shores.

Working for George Winkleblack meant a promotion out of the typing pool. This was the 70s— the upward mobility decade in California government. Goals were set for promoting women and minorities and I was one of each. I learned later from Bill, my former boss, that he was worried about my moving to the Mobile Equipment Unit. He never explained what concerned him and I didn't ask. But I did wonder. Did he think I would be offended by the salty language of the men? My Irish mother had inoculated me since birth. Was it a racial thing? Did he think the blue collar workers would become disoriented having a dark-skinned British secretary?

My transfer went smoothly. I got along with everyone—even John Hevron, the gruff superintendent whose men stood a little straighter when he made field inspections.

After a year working for George I was ready to move on. The day before I left to take the high-rise elevators to the 11th floor, George handed me a rectangle package carefully wrapped in brown paper and tied with string. It was a watercolor that he'd painted, and framed. I had no idea he was an artist. More surprising, the painting was of the rustic century old barn in the field next to my house.

I could feel my allergies acting up again.

I went onward and upward, and George eventually retired. We didn't stay in touch. Years later I was saddened to see George Winkleblack's name in the obituaries.

I'd hung George's watercolor in the house we'd retired to in the foothills. I remembered as I gazed at the painting one morning that it was the barn that had convinced us to settle on the ten acres. It certainly wasn't the house—a faded brown wooden structure with a flat roof. A real estate company had used it as an office in the city, then jacked it up and dropped it on the acreage. We'd sold the place to developers years ago.

Our daughter, Tina, a teenager at the time we bought the place, fell in love with the barn. She had a stable for the horse she'd been dreaming about for years. Raven, a Tennessee Walking Horse and Appaloosa mix, would occupy her time until the Pontiac Firebird stole her heart.

One autumn Raven shared the barn with half of our kid's senior high classmates as they spent late-September evenings under the dusty rafters building a homecoming float. Their laughter floated across the field and through my open window.

Now as I looked at the painting, the barn and the tall yellowed grass blurred. I remembered how much it meant that George took the time to drive out to the country and photograph our barn and then to paint it—just for me. I reached for the tissues on the dresser.

My allergies were acting up again.

****

'Till Death Us Do Part

November 1, 2017

I always thought my husband's fascination with reading the obituaries was a bit odd. Our morning conversations would go something like this:

"Did you know a John Davidson?" Jim would ask, focused on his favorite page.

"What agency did he work for?" I'd answer.

"It doesn't say. It just says the 'State of California.'"

I'd smile, hidden behind my opened newspaper thinking, "There are only several hundred thousand state employees. Why wouldn't I know him?

Jim's interest in the departed isn't morbid. He's simply curious about people's lives—the living as well as the dead. Sometimes he'd read aloud an unusually long obituary. It amazed us how much some people managed to cram into their lives. They ran businesses, volunteered at umpteen charities, received awards for this and that, and had hobbies galore. Jim and I would laugh and agree that if either of us was going to have anything substantive written about us, we'd better get cracking—NOW.

After listening to countless of these mini-biographies, I was inspired to make an offer one January morning. I volunteered to write my father-in-law's obituary.

Roger's passing was not sudden, nor thankfully, was it drawn out. He'd had a series of minor strokes throughout his life, and then, at age 85, a final one. I was confident I could put together highlights of Roger's life that would do him justice, and be acceptable to my husband and his family. Writing the obituary proved easier than finding a suitable photograph.

My father-in-law wasn't an expressive man, but I was still surprised at how stoic he looked in the stacks of photographs retrieved from the shoeboxes kept in a trunk in the basement and from the Cadbury's chocolate biscuit tin on the top shelf of the bedroom closet. I wanted to find a pleasing photo. Jim and I would cluck about some of the obituary photos that looked as if they had been selected by someone with a grudge against the departed. I eventually found a photograph I could use. Someone had coaxed a smile from Roger. He was even looking at the camera, his well-defined eyebrows arched above his horn-rimmed glasses.

My father-in-law looked younger than he was, even when he wasn't in the best of health. His body stayed muscular at an age when most were becoming frail, and then there was his hair. Each time Jim saw his dad, they would go through the same routine.

"Jim, you know what?"

"What, Dad?"

"I've still got my hair."

Both men would grin.

Much to his wife's chagrin, whose hair had both grayed and thinned decades earlier, Roger was well into his 70s before his thick, dark wavy hair began to thin and lose color. Jim had inherited his father's hair and was even voted, "Best Hair" in school.

As I studied Roger's photograph, I remembered how much he liked to tell stories. He often gave impromptu monologues at his club meetings. Occasionally the stories were off-color, or worse, involved a mimicked speech impediment. These performances mortified my mother-in-law. At one event Betty heard laughter as she exited the ladies room. Her worst fears were confirmed. Roger was standing at the podium. "I couldn't believe it," Betty said recounting the experience. "He was at it again. I made a quick about face to the powder room."

Sadly, there would be no more jokes from Roger. In early January he lay in a hospital bed with an off-white sheet pulled up to his chin, his eyes closed. Narrow, transparent plastic tubes were clipped inside his nose and taped to his motionless hands.

Betty sat next to his hospital bed in a recliner the nurse had brought in so she could elevate her feet. Betty looked as if she had been magically transported from the family room of the house she and Roger shared for 50 years. Her perfectly coifed head was bent as she peered through her stylish gold-rimmed glasses, her busy fingers crocheting something colorful.

There is a shiny oblong whiteboard on the wall to the right of the hospital bed. Before Roger's final stroke, he'd asked a nurse to write something on the board. It was a phrase he insisted on being displayed in each of the hospitals and care facilities he'd been admitted to over the years. I included it in the obituary:

"When I was in 6th grade, I pointed to Betty and told my friends, 'That's the girl I am going to marry.'"
The marriage lasted 65 years and 5 months.

Postscript: My father-in-law was the last of his five siblings to pass away, and at an older age. I credit his longevity to my mother-in-law who watched him like a hawk when he was in the yard wildly swinging a chain saw.

****

I Can See Clearly Now

December 14, 2017

People tell me I look pretty good for my age, and my five senses seemed to be working well. So you can understand how shocked I was when I heard this:

"Cataracts," announced my soft-spoken ophthalmologist.

I thought you had to be at least 100 years old before cataracts appeared. I'd seen little blue-haired ladies scrunched down in the passenger seat of passing sedans wearing those signature solid black wraparound sunglasses. I wasn't ready for that.

"You're ready," my doctor said as he referred me to a specialist.

Before I met with the eye surgeon, I hit the internet. I wish I hadn't. I scared myself. I thought the surgeon would magically access my cloudy lens, spray on a little Windex, and that would be that. Wrong.

Instead of poking around the internet and making myself nervous, I should have adopted the attitude of the parachute jumper: You're up in the clouds, the bay door is open. Now jump.

I jumped and off to my pre-op appointment, I went. I dutifully followed a technician from one small examination room to another. The surgeon popped in after the final test to explain the surgical procedure and answer my questions. He looked to be in his 50s.

Good, not too young, and not too old. He didn't smile.

Good, a serious man. I didn't need a comedian performing surgery on my eyes.

Everyone that I bored with talk about my up-coming surgery told me I would love the results. Three million people a year couldn't be wrong they said, and the 98 percent success rate they quoted was heartening.

I became even less anxious when I talked with family members. My father-in-law had cataract surgery decades earlier, with excellent results. He ended up with 20-20 vision and no longer needed glasses, even for reading. But family and friends were so used to seeing Roger with glasses they said his eyes looked beady without them. Roger took the comments with good humor but went back to wearing glasses, this time with non-prescription lenses.

The surgery on both of my eyes was successful, although I did have a couple of scares. Blood vessels broke in the same eye two separate times. The condition sounded life-threatening—a subconjunctival hemorrhage—that looked awful, but wasn't serious.

"Just in time for Halloween," my usually empathetic daughter, Tina, told me after I described my blood-filled eye.

The first bleeding occurred one week before the second operation. There was no warning. I looked in the bathroom mirror one morning and recoiled in horror. My eye was completely red. A visit to the surgeon's office confirmed I had nothing to worry about. I was so vain, though, I wore those wraparound dark glasses while indoors and frequently bumped into things.

The second bloody eye occurred a week after surgery. I telephoned my ophthalmologist. In his comforting way, he asked questions then advised me to call if things worsened.

They didn't.

What is it about talking to a doctor on the phone that makes you sit up straight and speak politely?

That call reminded me of visits by my childhood doctor in England. As soon as Dr. Carpenter walked into the house, my Irish mother developed a cultured English accent that would have made the Queen proud. Now I understood.

Despite all the rave reviews, I was unprepared for what I saw when I removed the eye patch the morning after my first surgery. Remember the opening scenes of "The Wizard of Oz" where the film starts in black and white in Kansas, and then transitions to color? Well, it wasn't quite that dramatic, but it was close.

On the walk to the front gate to pick up the newspaper I twirled around like a kid at Disneyland. The hazy veil from my eyes had been lifted. The pines and cedars looked greener; the sky was bluer, the clouds whiter and fluffier. I may have skipped back to my front door.

I made a mental note to send a thank you to my doctors and their staff. I have no memory of the surgery, but I remember that comforting heated blanket the pre-op nurse gently placed over me.

There were a few downsides to seeing more clearly—fingerprints all over my kitchen appliances, and cobwebs in every corner. I also looked younger the night before I removed the eye patch.

And a word to my husband:

"Jim, why didn't you tell me I had a little black hair sprouting from my chin?"

****

Discoveries

I t's not Buckingham Palace," my daughter teased—a reference to my English upbringing. We were in Washington D.C., travelling with Tina, her husband and their two friends. Tina had heard the White House was small and a little shabby. She didn't want me to be disappointed.

"I don't think people realize this is a house that's lived in," she went on with a hint of defensiveness.

We were all thankful the tour wasn't canceled. This was 2014 when President Obama was in office. The weeks preceding our trip there had been calamities, from fence jumpers to riots, that could have shut down the White House tours.

I wasn't disappointed by what I saw. I've toured European palaces and stately homes, and while these places were more grand, I loved the simplicity of the White House. The style fits the spirit of the New World—elegant, but not too royal.

A visit to D.C. wouldn't be complete without a punt on the Potomac. On the boat from Georgetown to Alexandria, we pointed like excited children to the magnificent monuments we had seen the night before.

From the boat dock, our group sauntered up the cobblestone hill to Alexandria's old town and stopped at the Visitor's Center. The petite, grey-haired woman behind the counter was helpful, but followed each of her suggested tourist sites with an "oops, it's closed today," or with a worried glance at the clock on the wall, exclaiming, "it closes in fifteen minutes." One place that was open for at least an hour, she told us enthusiastically, was the Apothecary Museum.

A white-haired docent with a charming southern accent greeted us from behind the museum's long marble counter. "This museum was originally a pharmacy—one of the oldest in the nation," he began. "It was founded in 1792 by Quakers, who, incidentally," he said, followed with a dramatic pause, "purchased slaves so they could set them free." Tina and I exchanged smiles.

Bottles of all shapes, colors, and sizes filled glass cases. "People would leave a lot happier than when they came in," the docent said pointing to a shelf of mysterious concoctions.

Our guide was an entertaining storyteller, his voice rising and falling for effect. My excitement mounted as we followed him up the narrow wooden stairs, and entered a small empty room. The docent paused, and with a flourish, turned and slowly slid open a door that looked like part of a wall.

We entered a wizard's workshop. I expected Harry Potter to pop up at any minute. Dusty hand-blown glass jars, once filled with secret potions, lined the shelves. Tiny drawers were stacked to the ceiling and labeled with herbal remedies that sounded more deadly than healthy. This was the apothecary manufacturing room.

The workshop looked exactly like it did when the pharmacy owner turned the key and walked away in 1933. This hidden treasure was only discovered a few years ago during restoration. The museum curator had the good sense to forbid any reorganization.

Before leaving D.C. we had one more place to visit: The Vietnam Veterans Memorial Wall. On our last evening, the six of us walked silently alongside the ten-foot-high black granite walls. Small circles of light from our miniature flashlights flickered across the etched names. We were searching for one name among the more than 58,000 soldiers who'd been killed, and the 1,200 who remain missing.

"What was the name again?" our daughter Tina asked her father, reaching into her purse for her iPhone.

"Eddie Butler," Jim said. "He was in the Marines."

Eddie was Jim's friend. As teenagers, they'd spent many lazy sunny afternoons fishing down at Erv's Boat Landing on the Sacramento River.

"How will we find him?" I asked, "There are thousands of names, and they're not in alphabetical order."

Tina began reading from her iPhone:

"PFC Edward Wayne Butler. Born on July 11, 1945, Sacramento, California. He died July 22, 1966."

"That's Eddie," said Jim, standing several panels away from the rest of us.

Marine Pvt. Edward W. Butler had enlisted in the Marines in October 1965 and was shipped to Viet Nam six months later. He served for three months before dying from a gunshot wound to his chest. He was 21 years old.

"He's on Panel 9E, Row 55," Tina said, scanning the black marble with her light. "Let's see where we are." She walked towards her father.

"I don't believe it. Dad's standing in front of Panel 9E."

The rest of us crowded next to Jim, and each shone a light up, down, and across the list of names.

"There he is," said Jim.

He reached out and touched his friend.

Marine Pvt. Edward W. Butler

Star

PERCEPTIONS

*When grouping my columns for publication, I wondered if my "**Best in Show**"—a first impression of a neighbor, and "**Gaming Grandma**"—understanding a grandson, had anything in common. The phrase "preconceived notions" came to mind.*

Best in Show

Watching the 141st Westminster Dog show reminded me of the first time I met my neighbor.

"I can't believe what just happened to me," I complained to my husband and went on to whine about the neighbor at the end of the road. She'd told me not to walk on her lawn after I took a short cut to the mailbox. This, mind you, was a lawn with a well-worn path strewn with undelivered newspapers. "I told her I was trying to avoid being roadkill, but I'd walk on the road from then on if it was a problem."

Weeks later, as I did my tightrope walk on the outer edge of her grass, praying that some lunatic driver making a wide left turn wouldn't disable me for life, my neighbor happened to be getting out of her car (parked on the lawn). Minutes before, as I passed the side of her house, a pack of tiny, hairy dogs greeted me with a variety of yips and yaps. They were bobbing up and down on the upper deck, desperately trying to keep me in their sights.

On impulse I walked over to her car. "Excuse me," I said, "I was wondering what breed of dogs you have? Once in a while they come tearing out on your deck to greet me when I walk by."

"Oh," she said smiling, "they're Yorkshire Terriers. I show them."

"Really," I responded.

"I've been doing this for years. I've won at least 70 awards. I used to travel all over the United States. In fact I've appeared at the Westminster Dog Show." I was impressed.

Donna introduced herself and invited me in for a cup of tea.

"How did you get started showing dogs?" I asked after I made myself comfy on her couch.

"I didn't start off intending to show," she'd replied, and told me the story of getting her first 'Yorkie' as a gift from a relative, and going on to purchase a registered terrier, then entering her first show in 1975.

I asked how a dog is judged.

"They look at the dog's disposition and temperament," Donna said, her voice taking on the tone of a teacher, "look at the dogs back to see that its level. Teeth are important—you want a good bite, not over or under. Ears are another important feature. They should stand straight up, not stick out to either one side or the other." Donna demonstrated the ear angle with her fingers. I stifled a giggle.

"The way the dogs walk matters—it's called 'angulation.' The judge will watch them walk away and turn and walk towards them."

"Steele blue is the optimum color. Someone told me that if you look down the barrel of a gun you'll see the perfect color for a Yorkshire Terrier's coat."

Donna then smiled and admitted she had no intention of looking down the barrel of a gun to confirm this.

My gaze drifted up to the imposing portrait hanging on the opposite wall. The background was bright pink and the Yorkie in the picture was a beautiful silken-haired puppy with a pink bow in her hair.

Donna followed my gaze. "That's Star," she said, her voice softening.

"She was the winner out of a group of 27 puppies. The contest was held in a New York hotel. I was next to the last to compete, so we had to wait a long time. I put Star on the table and the judge ran his hands over her. Then I walked her. One of the judges carried Star to a section of the room and positioned her under the natural light streaming from a skylight. Then the last dog was up. This dog had a lot of hair and was not really top quality, but they were giving it a lot of attention. Then the judge pointed to Star. She was judged number one. She won the grand sweepstakes, winner of the whole ball of wax. To top it off, her sister, who was one year older, won second place in a different category. I was so dazed by Star's win that I didn't quite comprehend her sister's achievement."

Donna shared another interesting tidbit.

In 1978, a Yorkshire Terrier won the coveted "Best in Show" at the Westminster Dog Show. Cede

Higgins was the first, and still the only Yorkshire Terrier, to ever win the title.

Unfortunately, Donna wasn't the owner of Master Higgins, but, she proudly proclaimed, a genealogy search confirmed that all her Yorkies were his descendants.

It's amazing what you can learn when someone tells you to get off her lawn.

****

Gaming Grandma

"They held a video game exhibition at Golden One Center," said my husband, Jim, peering over his newspaper. "Have you ever heard of such a thing?"

"I have," I replied smugly.

The lead-up to my education began at my daughter's house. Our grandson, Cameron, 17 years old at the time, sauntered into the living room wearing a robe. It was three o'clock in the afternoon.

"Did you just get up?" I asked accusingly.

"I was playing video games 'till about five in the morning," he responded with a slow smile, followed by a yawn. "Video games are fun, Grandma; you should play sometime."

"They're so violent; I wouldn't be able to stand it."

"They're not all violent. Come over sometime, and I'll show you."

"Okay, you're on," I heard myself saying. We arranged to meet in a couple of weeks.

"It'll be fun," he said, stifling another yawn.

Two weeks later Grandson answered the doorbell. His six-foot frame filled the doorway. He pulled a long, dark brown curl away from his face. He looked unusually clear-eyed. No doubt he got a few more hours of sleep in preparation for our video game competition.

Grandson sat beside me on the living room sofa and began describing his video game equipment.

"That's a Sony PlayStation 3," he said pointing to an oblong box that looked like my BlueRay disc player. "It's a generation 7. The generation 8 for Microsoft, the Xbox One, is just out." I appreciated he thought I knew what he was talking about.

"This is the controller," he continued as he placed the contraption in my hands. I'd seen these before, but had never held one.

"Put your thumbs on the analog sticks and your forefingers on the bumpers and triggers," he said, gently guiding my hand. "Just relax your fingers."

Cameron had chosen *Journey*, a simple game where the player controls a faceless figure in a robe and a scarf, crossing a hilly desert. When the player tags the scarf, the figure floats in the air and travels greater distances. Grandson explained how to handle the controls—what to press, and when. I've never been coordinated, but I managed to get the robed figure to do a couple of jumps.

"I have some others to show you, Grandma."

I followed Cameron into his bedroom. I braced myself—recalling snippets of conversation between Grandson and his mother that included the words: "Health Department."

The door opened freely. A snow blower's path had been cleared from the door to the computer chair.

"I'm going to show you StarCraft. I think you'll find this game interesting," Grandson said in all seriousness. I watched as a burst of colors and objects I couldn't identify flashed onto the monitor, followed by sporadic explosions.

"There are three competing races," Cameron explained. He went on to identify the strength and weakness of each race. I couldn't keep up with the action; things were blowing up in every direction. I finally understood these groups were separate armies on combat maneuvers trying to outflank and destroy each other.

I marveled at Cameron's ability to handle the controls, and think strategically—at warp speed. I declined his offer to play. He'd forgotten that when he was 5 years old, I'd refused his offer to teach me Chess.

It was then that he brought up video game tournaments.

"Did you know Grandma that professional players compete for six-figure prize money?"

"Never heard of that. How does that work?"

"Players sit on opposite ends of a stage in a tiny booth with windows, their faces blocked by large computer monitors. All the audience sees are their hands. The players keep one hand on the mouse and the other on the left of the keyboard so they can quickly reach the special hot keys.

"Players have speed ratings called APM's—actions per minute calculated on the number of actions a player performs. It's like a baseball player's pitching speed. Some gamers can average up to 1,000 APM's during a battle segment."

I silently compared this with my 45-words-a-minute typing speed.

Lesson over, I looked around the bedroom—books everywhere.

"Have you read all these?" I asked.

"Most of them. I like science fiction, but I've read lots of the classics. *The Glass Bead Game* is my favorite."

I walked over to his dresser and read aloud some of the titles: Siddhartha, Cat's Cradle, Foundation Series, Neuromancer, Jonathon Strange and Mr. Norrel, Le Morte D'Arthur, The Brothers Karamazov. The Fountainhead was the only book I'd read.

I'd have to remember to tell Grandpa that Grandson does something other than play video games. He reads books—some with titles I couldn't pronounce.

Cameron walked me to the front door.

"Thanks for coming, Grandma," he said as I hugged him. He smiled and, I noticed, didn't yawn.

Schuyler Colfax—17th Vice President of the United States (1869-1873). Served under General Ulysses S. Grant.

ABOVE THE FOG AND BELOW THE SNOW

It's been called "the drinking town with a railroad problem." Colfax, a city of less than 2,000 nestles in the Northern California foothills below the Sierra Nevada Mountains. A Union Pacific Railroad mainline runs through the center of town. If you drive slowly down Grass Valley Street past the train depot, you'll see a bronze statue of the town's namesake, Schuyler Colfax. He sits atop a brick pedestal, one hand behind his back, looking east to the mountains.

Colfax is my third California home, and hopefully will be my last. I've lived here for 14 years, and love it. The town reminds me of the small town in England where I grew up—a town where you pass people in the street who know your name.

The stories that follow inlude a tribute to the dedicated members of the Friends of the Colfax Library—featured in **"It Takes a Santa's Village,"** and **"A Wish for Santa,"**—and to the town's people in **"The Talent Show."**

It takes a Santa's Village

December 22, 2016

"Neither snow nor rain nor ..." begins the motto of the U.S. Postal Service, a saying that could easily be applied to a group of small-town volunteers.

Not once had the Friends of the Colfax Library cancelled their annual Santa's Village. Even the year the snow was so high that the parade was cancelled Santa jumped on his sleigh and slid into town. The year of my story, however, it was touch and go.

I began paying as much attention to the weather forecast as my husband does to football scores—

hoping for a winning pick. One day the prediction for Saturday was 30 percent chance of rain, another day it was torrential rain and wind, and yet another claimed dry by the afternoon!

I was on elf duty. Was this thing on or off? Emails flew. One contact said the whole Winterfest was off—no parade and definitely no fireworks.

Saturday morning I woke to the sound of pelting rain and howling wind. My husband, Jim, a reluctant volunteer at the best of times, said we should cancel. "Nobody is going to show up in this," he said. He's a retired construction supervisor—used to calling the shots when it came to the weather. If it was raining you called your men off—no hemming and hawing.

"I'm going to be at Roy Tom's Plaza at noon as planned. We'll see what happens." This was Chief Elf and Friends' President, Heidi Johnson, speaking. I got the message.

Despite his reluctance, Jim had joined volunteers Ron and Joe, and the three were staying dry under the gazebo on Main Street when I arrived. They stood among the boxes of decorations and rolled windbreak tarpaulins painted with Christmas scenes by local artist, Foxey McCleary. The four of us stared at the rain still coming down sideways. We were joined by Mayor Tom Parnham, and a young man named Travis. They had good news.

The owner of the Old Pharmacy building across the street had offered her place for the Santa event. Sherri Peterson pushed hard against the wind to open the door. I expected to enter a small empty shop. Instead, what lay before me was a room so long I could barely see the back wall—over two thousand square feet Sherri would tell me. A lighted Christmas tree stood in one corner almost touching the 15-foot ceiling. There was a comfy sofa and an easy chair beside the tree—perfect for Santa and Mrs. Claus. On the back wall was a neon light flashing "Uncle Sonny's." Sherri had spent a year converting this space into an event center that she'd named in honor of her late uncle.

I was glad I wasn't wearing my elf shoes. Now I could jump for joy without tripping over the curled toes, a frequent occurence. We would be inside—out of the rain and the wind.

Heidi arrived along with the rest of the elves— Sue, Teri, Gunda, Gayle, Barbara, and Joe. They cheerfully hauled bags and boxes out of trunks of cars into the dry, welcoming space.

Kevin, with his wife Karen assisting, set up the camera tripod. With the flair of Francis Ford Coppola, Kevin squinted through the lens and orchestrated the movement of just about everything. Santa was positioned on the couch. He would, as he has for fifteen years, listen patiently to the whispers of awed children. Mrs. Claus, who, it's rumored is overly friendly with the Mayor, perches on a chair to Santa's left—bags and baskets of gifts at her feet, including a gargantuan bin of candy-filled bags delivered by the Colfax Chamber of Commerce.

What would we do with all this stuff if nobody showed up?

Kelley Bernard-Garrett popped in while we were still setting up. Kelley's first visit with Santa had been a decade earlier. Her eldest son, Jayden, was five then and was now 15. Ethan was then three, and now thirteen. Three more children joined the Bernard-Garrett family: Ashlen, now eight, Carson, four, and Evlyn, three. Kelley promised to return with all five of her children. We knew at least one family would show up.

Vendors began setting up outside. Then we heard the parade would go on, and the fireworks would go off. The Soroptomists' Soup Kitchen at the Sierra Vista Center was packed. With a little encouragement from Mayor Tom, even the Christmas tree in Arbor Park would be lit.

The families came. There were infants swaddled around their mothers, babies in strollers and toddlers clutching dads' hands. Only a few cried when thrust at Santa. Most children squeaked out a grin, and some smiled so sweetly that onlookers let out collective "aah's."

What was that saying again: "Neither snow nor rain nor scary clown could stop Santa's Village from opening in town,"—or something like that.

****

A Wish For Santa

December 24, 2017

Roy Toms Plaza sits across the street from the string of shops that comprise Main Street.

For 15 years, a group of mostly women, members of the town's Friends of the Colfax Library group, have organized a Santa's Village in the Plaza's cabana during the town's Winterfest.

Most years, Santa and his entourage were protected from icy blasts blowing down from the Sierra Mountains by the canvas windbreakers decorated by local artist Foxie McCleary. But Foxie's cozy Christmas scenes couldn't protect Santa, Mrs. Claus or the elves on the severest winter nights.

One year they had the good fortune of being invited into the Old Pharmacy building, but that was a one-time deal.

So, the Friends' group were ecstatic when invited to move Santa's Village permanently into the warmth of the train depot waiting room across the street from the Plaza.

The day of the Winterfest the elf Friends arrived early to put the finishing touches to the decorations. A Christmas tree, wound with scarlet ribbons and dressed with glistening balls and snowflake ornaments, sparkled in one corner of the waiting room. Colorful holiday garlands were draped across windows and doors, transforming the monochrome waiting room into a festive workshop.

While the elves created a path of lights directing visitors to Santa's Village, my husband, Jim, and I were tasked with stringing the 6-foot Santa's Village banner on the plaza's arched entrance, a more visible spot than the train depot.

People who look like they have nowhere else to go often hang out in the plaza. That day two young men with an assortment of stuffed bags were standing by a bench outside the cabana. Each had long hair. One was fair-skinned and the other had a darker complexion and a bushy beard. Their appearance made me wary. As Jim struggled to tie the banner, the men asked if he needed help. As they came closer they looked less threatening. They were handsome, clear-eyed and smiling. They climbed the arch's metal steps with ease, and quickly tied the banner in place.

Jim and I thanked them and the four of us chatted for a bit. They had met, they said, on the train that had just arrived in Colfax from Colorado. The fair-haired guy introduced himself as Alexander and said he was a touring musician on his way to Los Angeles, but first had to get to Sacramento. The other man, whose name I've forgotten, was waiting for his girlfriend to drive up from Auburn. As we talked,

Alexander opened his guitar case, which was leaning against one of the bags, and fished out a music CD.

"What's your name," he asked, then scribbled a greeting on the back of the disc. I gave him some money as thanks. On my way back to the depot, I offered to show him where the bus to Sacramento stopped. As Alexander and I crossed the street, the dark-haired young man with the beard sailed by us, his long legs extended like a graceful gazelle. Running towards him was a pretty young woman. They embraced and lingered in a passionate kiss. Alexander turned to me and said with a wry smile, "Must be the girlfriend."

At the depot I introduced Alexander to Swen and his wife, Chris, members of the Colfax Historical Society who were volunteering in the museum adjacent to the waiting room. They welcomed Alexander and found a bus schedule for him.

When our Friends' group began planning the move from the Plaza, several members had fretted that people wouldn't be able to find us or that they wouldn't want to leave Main Street, the route of the parade of lights, and site of the vendor booths.

We needn't have worried. Kevin, the photographer who has donated his time and expertise for almost ten years, and his wife, Karen, patiently coaxed smiles from the more than 200 children who managed to find Santa. Each child left with a gift bag donated by the members of the

Friends, and a new book purchased with grant funds.

I rarely see Santa while he's chatting with the children. My elf station is outside and that's where I hand out envelopes to parents so they can receive their Santa photos. So, I didn't know that some children give Santa a personal note. As we were packing up for the night, I collected a bundle of letters that Santa had carefully placed by his bag. Karen was standing beside me as I opened the letter on top. In red crayon on white paper, a tiny hand had printed that they loved Santa. But it was the last words that brought tears to our eyes: "Please bring my daddy home."

It was left to our imagination whether the plea was for a daddy who was in the military, or one who had somehow left the family

Either way, I hoped he would find his way home.

****

The Talent Show

November 22, 2017

"Gramma, I'm too tired to go," whined my adult grandson when I invited him to attend a talent show at the Colfax Theater that evening. He claimed his overweight cat, Hope, had kept him awake the night before. I thought all-night video games might be involved. I decided to go alone.

The talent show was being held in the 1939 art deco movie house on Main Street. The theater had been bought and sold a number of times, and was vacant for eight years during one period. When I'd pass the empty cinema I'd silently pledge to support events if it ever opened again. When a well-known cinematographer purchased the theater I was as excited as a kid and scanned the building's neon marquee for upcoming events.

Five months before the theater was scheduled to reopen, however, the new owner suddenly died. The boarded-up building looked even sadder than before. Less than a year later, an article in the *Colfax Record* announced a Colfax resident, with ties to the San Francisco music scene, had purchased the theater. The new owner was the topic of conversation in the local Café Luna. Once again the community became energized.

Knowing this history, I was happy to see the crowd gathered outside the theater excited to watch the talent show. Children were jumping up and down as if they'd been bitten, while their parents ignored them and engaged in animated conversations with other big people.

Inside, a young man with tattooed forearms and dark hair standing straight up, exchanged my $5 for a paper bracelet bestowing in-and-out privileges. I nudged my way through the throng at the refreshment stand clamoring for popcorn and other refreshments to sustain them throughout the 90-minute show.

The theater was packed and loud. Adult voices mingled with children's squeals as the kids ran in and out of the aisles. I held onto the wooden rail and cautiously climbed the carpeted steps, surveying each row. I'd barely settled into the aisle seat when a middle-aged woman in a sleeveless dress and enviable toned upper arms, scooted by me and sat down. She introduced herself and asked to share my program. We both exclaimed surprise that there were 29 acts. As we chatted I reminded myself that going places alone could be fun. I may not have met this woman had my grandson joined me.

The crowd hushed as Rita Dolphin, the theater's community relations person at the time, appeared on stage sparkling like Cinderella's fairy godmother. Rita opened the show with a rousing, "There's No Business like Show Business." The girl could sing! The audience responded with enthusiasm—clapping and whistling their approval. Next up was Mary Price singing "Getting to know You" while scooping up a steady stream of little children who ran onto the lower stage chased by frantic parents.

The rest of the singers were not as experienced as Rita and Mary, but they sang with gusto. One soloist, a slender elderly woman, walked slowly onto the stage clutching a miniature schnauzer. Standing in front of the microphone with the dog clutched under her right arm, and a piece of paper in her left hand, she began to sing, "How much is that doggie in the window." Squinting at the paper, she sang the first line, and then stopped, as did John, the keyboardist. The singer repeated the first line, and then stopped again. The musician started playing, doing his best to prompt the singer who stumbled through the rest of the song, repeating some lines, and missing others. Her performance was one of the most endearing renditions of the song I have ever heard. The audience agreed, clapping loud and long.

A young ballerina then gave a polished performance entirely en pointe. A gymnast was breathtaking, both in quality and daring—her somersaults ended within inches of the speakers on the stage. The "Hot Tamales," four women of indeterminate age and hair color, performed a lively professional-quality rendition of familiar songs that brought the house down.

On the drive home I thought about the evening's performances. I had enjoyed the talent show, but realized it was the audience that impressed me the most. They spontaneously, and enthusiastically clapped, cheered and hooted for every single performer. I've never witnessed a more generous outpouring of support.

Rita had named the event "Colfax Got Talent." I chose to think of the show as "Colfax Got Heart."

෨෨

Downtown Reno, Nevada circa 1940s-50s

BIGGEST LITTLE CITY

The three stories that follow: **"Ride this Train,"** *"False Advertising" and "The Greatest Race" feature Reno, Nevada, a city located less than two hours northeast of my home in California. If it had not been for the American immigrant tradition of anglicizing surnames, Reno might very well have been called Renault—the ancestral name of Jesse Lee Reno, a soldier killed in battle in 1862, and after whom the city is named. I'd heard of Reno long before I immigrated to America. It was infamous for its liberal* *divorce laws. From the 1930s to the early 1960s, one half of a sparring couple needed only to live in Nevada for six weeks to qualify for the residency requirement prior to divorce proceedings.*

According to William L. McGee and Sandra V. McGee, authors of a number of books about Reno, Nevada offered nine grounds for divorce: impotency, adultery, desertion, conviction of a felony, habitual drunkenness, neglect to provide the common necessities of life, insanity, living apart for three years, and extreme cruelty entirely mental in nature. No proof was required of any of these.

Mental cruelty was the most popular charge and covered such egregious behavior as "she talks to me when I'm trying to read" or, my favorite, "he interrupts me when I'm trying to write."

Ride This Train

As expected, the Amtrak train to Reno was over an hour late arriving in Sacramento where my daughter, Tina, planned to board. I'd get on at the next stop in Colfax.

The train delay in Sacramento turned out to be a blessing in disguise. My daughter is a delight to travel with, but she is often late for appointments. When I called to check on her, I learned she was stuck in traffic. A big rig had overturned blocking traffic for several miles. I was relieved when she called to tell me she had boarded.

After depositing the luggage in our room at Reno's Silver Legacy Hotel, we headed for the restaurants. On our way, Tina spotted an advertisement for the Twelve Irish Tenors appearing at the neighboring Eldorado showroom. "Do you think it will make you cry," my daughter asked kindly, thinking about her Irish grandmother who had passed away. I shook my head. I'd read they sang a variety of songs, not just the mournful Irish ones.

Despite the claim the Twelve Irish tenors were "twelve of Ireland's finest," they turned out to be an eclectic bunch. One tenor had a very strong British accent having been raised in England; another is an Irish-American; another lived in Canada; and another had been born and raised in the Netherlands. Had they not confessed their nationalities the audience would never have guessed they were not truly Irish. They sang with gusto and harmonized beautifully.

As we entered the casino after the show, I thought of a quote from Dante's Inferno, "All hope abandon ye who enter here."

Ignoring the mental warning I skipped merrily over to the Wheel of Fortune slot machine knowing that I might as well open a window and throw my money into the Truckee River.

Perhaps it's the chance to "spin the wheel" that makes playing the Wheel of Fortune more fun than just pressing a button, or pulling the arm of what was once appropriately named the "one-armed bandit." I lost money, of course, then kept going beyond the limit I had set.

Tina, meanwhile, was bonding with a raucous group of craps shooters. Since she had studied the in-room video on casino games, she was feeling confident. She tried explaining the game to me, but I got lost at the "pass, no pass line." I told her I was sticking to the "Wheel of Fortune."

Across the room from Tina I continued to feed my insatiable machine, even forcing money back in the slot after it had been spat out.

"This is a sign" I would say to myself when the machine spat back my twenty-dollar bill for the second time. Well it's not called an addiction for nothing. I stuffed the money back in and continued playing. I was beginning to come to my senses and prepared to quit when a five times something appeared and the credits kept rolling, and rolling. I had won 2,000 quarters—$500.

Tina came up behind me as the credits were rolling. Since I never win anything, I hurriedly hit the "cash out" button and gave her permission to smack me if I as much as looked at another machine.

It was a great way to end our last evening, and still early enough to get a decent night's sleep before we boarded the train in the morning.

I had warned my daughter about the return train from Reno. The last time I rode this train it had arrived very late. Our train was scheduled to leave at 9:15 a.m., but that evening we received a message announcing the train wouldn't arrive until 11 a.m. We happily changed our wake up call for a later time. The next morning we called to confirm the 11 a.m. arrival time, but were informed the train had been delayed once again. It was now scheduled to arrive in Reno at 3:30 p.m., six hours later than originally scheduled.

"Are we still in America or did we get transported to a third world country in the middle of the night," Tina quipped. We both laughed and decided to make the most of our extra time in Reno—anything that didn't involve gambling. I knew my winnings would get sucked back in a heartbeat.

"What about a movie," Tina suggested. We agreed to go see, "Notes from a Scandal," starring the superb British actress Judi Dench.

"There's an auto museum here too," I said, as Tina leafed through the hotel's "What to do in Reno" book. We discovered the museum was just a few blocks from the movie theater so off we scampered. While it was cold outside, the morning was dry and sunny. We linked arms and focused on our good fortune with the weather, rather than our frustration with the train.

Tina was not as impressed with the movie as I, but we were both pleasantly surprised by the museum. We were limited to a whirlwind tour knowing that we could never live down missing a train that was six hours late!

We arrived at the station around three o'clock and settled in for the thirty minute wait. The station began to fill up with passengers, their faces revealing a range of discontent. One woman decided to ease her frustration by slamming down beers from her ice chest that alternated as a seat and a communal bar. Three-thirty came and went, as did four-thirty. The train chugged into the station just before 5—almost eight hours after its original arrival time.

We both had eaten a light lunch and were starving by the time we boarded. Tina went straight to the dining car to make reservations. She came back rolling her eyes.

"They are not taking reservations," she said through pinched lips. "They plan to open up at seven on a first-come first-served basis."

We decided to ward off starvation by getting some nuts and wine from the snack bar. Tina came back with a tray.

"I'm Tina, and I'll be your server," she said smiling mischievously as she pulled down the tray from the back of the seat.

A woman from across the aisle leaned over and said how sorry she was that we had to wait so long for the train, as if she were personally responsible for the delay.

"I boarded in Salt Lake City after waiting three hours," she said, in an effort to share our pain.

Strangers talked freely back and forth across the aisle recounting their experiences and expressing their frustrations. There was a sudden jolt as the train started.

As the train pulled out of the station, a faint message crackled over the intercom.

"I don't believe this—just great—the train whisperer," my daughter said sarcastically. Everyone within earshot laughed.

The staff had bellowed a series of inconsequential instruction as we boarded. Now we were straining to hear important arrival times—critical for those who had transportation connections.

In an attempt to mollify what was increasingly looking like a mutinous mob, all aboard were offered a complimentary meal of stroganoff.

"Well," I sniffed, "that's at least something."

Tina and I edged our way to the dining car and waited for our meal. I haven't owned a dog for several years, but I still remember what Alpo dog food looks like. So much for the complimentary stroganoff.

We moved the food around the bowl then left. It was time for another drink.

Not only was the train running late, it stopped enroute for mysterious reasons. I arrived at the Colfax depot at 10:30 p.m., more than 10 hours late.

My daughter still had two more hours before she arrived in Sacramento.

The next morning I got a call from Tina. "How are you?" I said.

"Well," she replied, "You obviously haven't checked your e-mail."

"What's going on?" I asked, expecting more horror stories about the remainder of her train ride.

The day before, Tina had walked the five blocks from the parking garage to the Sacramento train station. She had expected to arrive back in Sacramento while it was still daylight. Now it was past midnight when she returned, and Tina wisely took a taxi to the parking garage.

"I was in the taxi on the way to my car. We were driving across J Street when out of nowhere a speeding car hit the rear end of the taxi spinning us into a 360-degree turn," she explained. "The taxi flew up and over a curb, hit a tree, and came to a stop crashing into the corner of a building."

"Oh my God," I yelled into the phone, "Are you alright?"

Fortunately, neither Tina nor the taxi driver was hurt. Two police cars and two fire engines arrived on the scene. "It must have been a slow night," Tina quipped. Another taxi arrived and took her to the parking garage. Unfortunately, the taxi took off before Tina gathered her thoughts enough to ask the driver to stay while she entered the garage.

Here she was, alone, with a heavy suitcase, standing outside a deserted parking garage at 1:30 a.m. Deserted, that is, except for a row of homeless people peeking sleepily out of their sleeping bags.

"I flipped open my cell phone," Tina continued, " and thought I'm dialing 911 if they as much as cough in my direction. I was so relieved to get into my car and lock the doors."

"Mom," she said, softening her voice, "when I got into that first taxi I heard your voice. Remember when the snow shoe guide moved us from one SUV to another? You said you were glad we were riding in the newer vehicle because it had shoulder harnesses. I normally don't buckle my seat belt for a short taxi ride, but your voice echoed in my head. I reached over and put on my seat belt and shoulder harness."

As I was listening to Tina and feeling relief she wasn't hurt, I thought back on how often I would will that protective blanket over her and my two sons. Their first day starting school; the teenage years when they drove down the driveway; when the boys went away to college, and when Tina flew to France to live with a family we had never met.

"Just let me live long enough to see them grown up," I used to silently pray.

Now they are all grown, and I still want to live.

****

117

False Advertising

I'm big on taking lessons, so I was excited to find a snowshoe clinic that allowed customers to "set their own pace," and offered lunch. I hoped the class would inspire me to get more use out of the snowshoes I'd purchased years ago and used twice. My daughter, Tina, joined me.

The clinic was scheduled for 11:30 a.m., the morning after we arrived in Reno. John, the instructor, had offered us either an 8:30 a.m. or an 11:30 a.m. session. I chose 11:30 a.m. I got a call from him just as our train was pulling into the Reno station. Something had changed. He now only offered one session and would pick us up at 8:30 a.m. I was too busy getting off the train to protest.

There were no outdoorsy-looking people roaming our hotel lobby the next morning, so Tina and I took the elevator to the valet parking area. Tina phoned John. We could have called out his name. He was in a minibus looking at us through the windshield.

Our guide looked every bit the outdoorsy, adventurous type—Nordic features, fading tan, muscular—although he was carrying more weight than you'd expect of an athlete *All the better to piggyback me down the mountain.*

John gave me a polite hello, but his face lit up when he got a look at Tina. My daughter, who was in her early 40s at the time, is the only person I know who can look attractive first thing in the morning wearing a woolen snow cap with false pigtails. John informed us he was picking up a group of snowmobilers and Tina and I would be riding with his partner, Darren.

A soft snow was falling when we arrived just above North Star in Lake Tahoe. Darren pulled up beside John's minibus that was packed to the headliner with middle-aged couples wearing super-sized down jackets. John explained there'd be a short wait while he organized the snowmobilers since their rented vehicles were on a schedule.

The "snowshoe clinic" seemed a bit rushed. It consisted of John telling us we should always carry a whistle in the outdoors because if people can't see you, at least they can hear you. He also suggested carrying a shovel in case one needed to build a snow cave. Personally, I would have liked a tad more information if I were actually going to undertake this task. Carry matches or a lighter too he cautioned, and pay attention to where the sun is so you can judge your direction of travel. Then we were off.

It was straight uphill. John had the thighs of a speed skater and took off like a shot with Tina right behind him. I followed Tina with Darren following me. I consider myself reasonably fit, but I was soon out of breath. "I'm sorry," I'd say turning to Darren, "but I have to stop once in a while." I was wondering what happened to the brochure's "set your own pace" promise that had lured me to this clinic.

Tina and John would occasionally stop and wait for us. As we reached them, John would immediately take off. At one stop, Tina, noticing her mother's tongue was hanging out, suggested they wait so I could rest. John would frequently check his watch, and it dawned on me his frenzied pace was tied to the snowmobilers' rental schedule.

The clinic fee included "food and beverages," and when the four of us stopped for lunch John gallantly retrieved a small circular plastic disc from his backpack for me to sit on. Alas, the only food plucked from his bag was trail mix. My daughter kindly mentioned there was some tasty stuff mixed in with the nuts and raisins. The guide beamed. He said he had indeed added some extra items

I was glad he wasn't looking in my direction.

The trip down the hill was a lot more enjoyable. The weather had cleared, and the snow hung in puffs on the pine branches. Other than the noise and fumes from the snowmobilers, it was just lovely.

John had warned us he was upping the pace so he could get down the hill in time to meet his other group. Halfway down he broke into a gallop. The three of us almost lost our balance laughing at the sight of this large muscular guy flailing downhill in snowshoes. Tina demonstrated John's ungainly running technique. Darren got caught up in the fun and gave us his imitation. I was not about to follow suit. I had succeeded in my one goal—to remain upright.

While the clinic didn't inspire me to snowshoe more often, I did buy a whistle and a shovel.

****

The Greatest Race

February 18, 2018

My husband, Jim, recently said farewell to something he valued almost as much as he does me; the 1966 candy apple red Chevy Super Sport he purchased when he was 18 years old. The loss was tempered by the fact he sold it to Matt, a friend who lives near Colfax, and who plans to restore it. Jim has been given visitation rights.

For another auto fix, we traveled up Interstate 80 to Reno's National Automobile Museum on the banks of the Truckee River. The museum houses more than 200 cars dating from 1892 to the present. My favorite is the American 1907 Thomas Flyer, an entrant in the New York to Paris automobile race—a story that fascinates me.

Six cars—one each from America, Italy, and Germany, and three from France—started their engines in Times Square on Lincoln's Birthday in 1908. Thousands gave a rousing sendoff to what became the most incredible car race the world has ever seen.

The New York Times and the *Le Matin,* a Paris newspaper, sponsored the race. Each car had a team of three men. The American group comprised: George Schuster, age 35; Montague Roberts, 24, and Harold Brinker, 21. A correspondent from *The New York Times* rode with the American crew. His daily dispatches were front page news for nearly six months. While en route by ship, the reporter used carrier pigeons to fly stories back to Seattle. The articles were then telegraphed on to New York City.

Although E.R. Thomas entered a car in the race, he was one of the many skeptics. He doubted that any of the automobiles would make it past Chicago, let alone make it to Paris. *The London Daily Mail,* echoing the prevailing sentiment of the time—that horses were more reliable—pondered. "...the motor car, after a woman, is the most fragile and capricious thing on earth." With attitudes like those, you can understand why it took 12 more years for women to earn the right to vote in the United States.

The racers began their journey fighting freezing temperatures and blinding snowstorms on their way to Chicago. With no roads to speak of, the automobiles would often ride the rails, straddling the railroad tracks. Teams of horses would act as modern-day snowplows, pulling the vehicles through the blizzards.

The Thomas Flyer was the first to arrive in San Francisco, the first automobile to cross the entire United States in winter. Two of the three French motors didn't make it to the West Coast. One car broke down in Iowa, and the other conked out after traveling a mere 44 miles.

From San Francisco, the cars were supposed to board a ship to Anchorage and drive across Alaska. The organizers envisioned driving over frozen rivers and dog sled trails to the Bering Strait, then on to Siberia. Snowdrifts more than ten feet deep forced the Thomas Flyer to return to Seattle where it was transported by ship to Japan. After driving across the width of the island (the first car ever seen in that country), it was shipped from Japan to Vladivostok, Russia, for the trek across frozen Siberia to St. Petersburg, to Berlin, and finally to Paris.

One newspaper described this incredible feat as a "Skidding, shoveling, sleet-stinging, snow-clogging war against winter and it was a rain-drenching, mud-sinking battle against spring."

The teams battled the bone-chilling weather, appalling road conditions, and physical exhaustion—often going days without food or rest. The seatbelt in the Thomas Flyer was a man's belt nailed to the rider's seat. It was designed to keep the sleeping passenger from falling out of the car.

If the Thomas team thought their arrival in Paris meant their adventures were over, they were mistaken. A gendarme stopped them. They only had one headlight and were also required to pay a gasoline tax before they could proceed. The team was able to scrape together the tax money. A passing cyclist offered his lamp but then couldn't unbolt it from the bike. George hoisted the bike onto the hood and proceeded to the finish line at the Eiffel Tower. The American car was declared the winner.

The Thomas Flyer, with its 45-star American flag billowing from the rear, arrived in Paris on July 30, 1908. This incredible journey covered three continents and more than 22,000 miles over 169 days.

An ecstatic New York City crowd gave George Schuster and his team a ticker tape welcome home. Teddy Roosevelt, the first President to drive an automobile, invited the team and the Thomas Flyer to join him at his summer White House on Long Island.

For 110 years the Thomas Flyer has held the world record for this magnificent feat.

The Pyramids of Euseigne Switzerland
and the Spanish Steps in Rome.

ROME AND ROMANO

I'm a reluctant traveler, but after a glass or two of Klinker Brick's Old Vine at the Monte Vista, I convinced myself a few more trips across the pond was a good idea.

125

*"**Are these the Spanish Steps,**" chronicles my first and, so far, only trip to Rome. It was also the first vacation I've taken with two lady friends.*

*"**What's a Raclette?**" details my second visit to Switzerland with family. The first visit comprised a breezy trip on Lake Geneva before moving on. On this second visit we were able to stop and eat.*

Are these the Spanish Steps?

October 12, 2017

So there I was with my friend, Irene, entering the double doors of the 16th-century palazzo we'd rented in the heart of Rome.

Our apartment was on the fourth floor. We'd been warned there was no elevator. What we didn't know was that each flight was eight steps, a small landing, then 8 more steps—48 in all. Irene and I were in our late sixties and lugging 50-pound suitcases.

Our friend, Heidi, who'd arrived earlier, suggested we walk backward up the steps making it easier to lift our bags. Halfway up the second flight, I made the mistake of grabbing the metal stair rail. As I stooped to hoist my bag the support post came loose from its crumbling hole in the wall. It hit me on the head. I let out a yell—more from surprise than pain.

Heidi shushed me. She was worried about disturbing the tenants. After a ten-hour sleepless flight from San Francisco to London, a four-hour layover, a two-hour flight to Rome, an hour's ride from the airport, a smack on the head from a metal rail—being sensitive to invisible neighbors at ten at night, when most Italians were just starting dinner, was *not* high on my list.

This was my first visit to Rome. I think Irene had been to Rome once, years ago. Heidi loves the city—goes every year. She had another trip planned and chatted enthusiastically about it that night at Monte Vista. Her excitement was infectious. Irene and I decided to tag along.

Our first morning in the Rome apartment we lounged in nightgowns on the rooftop patio off the kitchen—hair in various stages of disarray. Heidi and I munched on granola, and Irene nibbled on McVities' English biscuits and sipped Ty-phoo tea from a personal stash. Irene and I grew up in England and referred to each other as city mouse and country mouse—a mutual mocking of her London East End birthplace, and my East Midlands upbringing. I'd long ago given up tea and biscuits for breakfast.

We had a stunning view from the patio—the cloisters of an ancient monastery, ornate church domes, and tile rooftops home to pigeons and some outspoken gulls. From where I sat I could see something hanging above Irene's bed in the attic bedroom. Irene explained that she had gotten up several times during the night. What I saw dangling, she'd said nonchalantly, was her orange silk scarf. Irene had hung it on the sloped ceiling beam to avoid hitting her head for the third time.

Recovered, rested and ready to go, Irene and I followed Heidi around the city's winding cobblestone streets. Heidi knew where to go and how to get there. The city was beyond beautiful— plazas with magnificent statues and fountains around every corner. We marveled at ancient ruins and tiptoed through spectacular churches. I gasped when I saw the Roman Colosseum, tossed coins over my shoulder into the Trevi Fountain, and got a neck ache admiring Michelangelo's frescoes on the ceiling of the Sistine Chapel.

Rome, as everyone knows, is famous for its aqueducts and ancient baths, which is why I asked myself this question. Who designed their public restrooms? Some toilets had levers, some had either a small or large square button depending on the event, and some had a chain just like the outdoors lavatory where I grew up. Wash basins were another surprise. I kept forgetting the "C" on a faucet did not mean cold, but stood for "Caldo"—meaning hot. I spent a good ten minutes trying to turn on a tap in one bathroom only to discover floor pedals operated the water.

My first experience with a toilet outside the apartment was in a cafe in the Palazzo Farnese. The bathroom was down a curved flight of stairs with a low roof. On my way to the toilet, I saw two bright red and black warning stripes painted on the sloped ceiling. I didn't notice any on my way back. I smacked my head. I sheepishly told my friends, and Irene admitted to doing the same. She and I now had several head bangs each.

Thanks to our intrepid guide, Heidi, we saw every site we wanted to see. We even climbed the steep slope between the Piazza di Spagna and the Piazza Trinita dei Monti—known as the Spanish Steps. There are 138 of them.

"Gluttons for punishment" my mum would've said.

****

What's a Raclette?

It was while I was admiring the Alpine scenery on a train ride from Geneva to Sion, a city in southwestern Switzerland, that I remembered a YouTube video where Conan O'Brien interviewed Anthony Bourdain.

Bourdain is a famous American chef and television personality. In his television show he travels around the world "uncovering lesser known places and exploring cultures and cuisine."

Wikipedia notes that Bourdain has eaten, among other things: "a raw seal eyeball...an entire cobra—beating heart, blood, bile, and meat." There were other "delicacies" listed, but they're too disgusting to mention.

But it wasn't Bourdain's bizarre appetites that came to mind on that Swiss train; it was a comment he made to O'Brien. Bourdain confessed to a "morbid fear of everything Swiss." He blamed his phobia on the movie, "The Sound of Music," which somebody should have told him was filmed in Austria. He abhorred the Tyrolean hat with its feathers, and described yodeling as "horrifying." In another interview, he disparages lederhosen, cuckoo clocks and even knocks Ricola Swiss cough drop commercials, which apparently make him "break into a cold sweat." If all this isn't bizarre enough, he can't stand the cheese. Yes, the cheese.

I burst out laughing when I heard his comments. The man has chronicled visits to 16 countries, some of them during hostilities, including Beirut, Mozambique, The Congo, Kurdistan, Libya, and Haiti during a cholera threat.

Could there be a more sedate country than Switzerland? This is the land of clocks and watches and delicious chocolate, where the trains run on time, and the people are purported to be orderly, law-abiding, and who mind their own business at all costs.

With these thoughts swirling, I stepped off the train in Sion and was greeted with smiles and hugs by Jeane and George, our California neighbors who'd invited us to spend a couple of nights at their summer home.

The house was no rustic chalet. Jeane had worked with an architect to include unique features, such as arched and diagonal entrance ways. I couldn't see a straight line anywhere. The doors were handmade from exotic wood. Light streamed in through large windows. Each one offered a glimpse of the Swiss Alps. Ornate glass sculptures reflected on shining tabletops throughout the house. Despite its elegance, the house felt warm and welcoming. I knew everything would be fine as long as I didn't trip.

We spent the only full day of our visit on a leisurely drive around the nearby towns dotted with picture-postcard chalets. The Alpine scenery was breathtaking. Anthony Bourdain would have been taken ill.

In a nearby village, gigantic conical rock formations stretched toward the sky, each topped with a huge boulder. They're known as the Pyramids of Euseigne. The unique shape of the rocks evolved over the years, carved and degraded by the rainfall.

Sightseeing stimulated our appetites and prompted our hosts to pull into the parking lot of "Relais des Reines," their favorite local restaurant. Once we were seated, Jeane asked Jim and me to pick one of the restaurant's two famous dishes: the fondue or the raclette. Since we were familiar with fondues, we went for the raclette.

As it turns out, we were dining in the canton of Valais where the raclette dish originated. The story goes that in the summer months, Swiss shepherds from Valais, a French-speaking region, brought cheese and potatoes up to the Swiss Alps because they wouldn't spoil. They roasted potatoes in an open pit and placed hunks of cheese next to the fire. When melted, the cheese was scraped onto the baked potatoes. "To racler" is French for "to scrape." *Voila,* the Raclette was born.

In the Sion restaurant, I wandered over to the spot the waiter had suspended a huge round of cheese over the raclette, a grill that takes the place of the shepherds' open fire. The melted cheese was delivered to our table with baskets of small, hot boiled potatoes. The meal was delicious and filling. I sat back expecting the waiter to remove my plate. Instead, he returned to our table with another serving of cheese and another basket of potatoes.

Two more servings would follow—each with a different variety of cheese. All four of us had difficulty standing at the end of the meal. Back in the car, there was unanimous agreement that a mandatory hike was in order.

Maybe Anthony Bourdain was on to something.

Postscript: Sadly, Anthony Bourdain, a gifted chef and storyteller, took his own life in France on June 8, 2018.

Island of Poquerolle, France

FRENCH CONNECTION

Our French connection began in 1980. I was very pregnant when our sixteen-year-old daughter, Tina, who had previously convinced me to buy a wig I didn't need, talked me into hosting a French exchange student named Cedric. Despite my husband's fear that I was jeopardizing the health of the pregnancy by inviting a stranger into our home, Cedric was a delight, and became my husband's fishing buddy.

A few years later, Cedric returned the hosting favor by inviting Tina to France. That visit inspired Tina to major in French in college, and then journey back to France where she intended to live for a few years.

Tina couldn't find regular employment. France, at the time, required that non-citizens had to prove they were providing a service unavailable from a French person. Her funds dwindled. She became depressed, and seriously considered abandoning her dream of staying in France.

One morning, while crossing a pedestrian bridge in the city of Lyon, Tina was approached by an aggressive panhandler purporting to represent a charitable organization. Tina explained that she didn't have any money. The panhandler responded by berating her, making lewd gestures, and blocked her from walking on. Tina was near tears when a passing young French woman came to her aid, shouting to the panhandler to leave Tina alone. At the Metro station, Tina and the young woman met again. The Good Samaritan was named Marie, and she knew someone who needed a live-in housekeeper. Tina had found work and a home.

Years later, Tina would be the maid of honor at Marie's wedding, and the godmother of her youngest daughter. They have been close friends for more than 30 years.

My husband and I have been embraced by Marie, her husband, Renee, and their families. We've spent wonderful vacations at their home in the small country village of Vignieu.

*The stories that follow describe some of the memorable times I've spent with Marie and her family: There's Marie's neighbor's surprising 50th birthday in "**Cracking the Whip**;" a reminder of why I stay away from the water in "**Snorkeling with Orlando Bloom**;" celebrating Bastille Day in "**What Doesn't Kill You**," and excerpts from Marie's Uncle Wisse's cross-country cycling adventure in "**Brooklyn to Bodega Bay**."*

Cracking The Whip

Whenever we drove up the hill to Marie's house in Vignieu, an ancient village in the southeast of France, I'd squint through the dusty side window of the Peugeot. Each time I'd hope their neighbor's wooden gates that stood as tall as nearby trees, would open.

"You're all invited to Jean-Paul's 50th birthday party on Sunday."

Marie was speaking to me, my husband, Jim and our daughter and son-in-law, Tina and Brian. The five of us were sitting around the kitchen table sipping frothy coffee from gigantic white mugs. We'd never met Marie's neighbor, Jean-Paul, but he must have heard "the Americans," as we were known, were visiting. Now I'd get to solve the mystery of what was behind those massive garden gates.

Sunday afternoon, joined by Marie's husband, Renee, the six of us trooped down the hill. The gates were open. I should have entered in a carriage. The property looked like the grounds of an English stately home. There were acres of plush grass, broad-trunk trees thick with leaves and masses of bushes sagging with colorful blooms. As I dawdled behind Marie on our way to the house, we passed a glistening swimming pool that seemed out of place in the bucolic surroundings.

Two plump women wearing aprons hustled between picnic tables placing leafy sprigs and blossoms along the center of the blue, white, and red table covers—the colors of the French flag.

A makeshift wooden buffet table circled the base of a huge oak tree. Several blue-striped, scalloped-edged canopy tents—insurance against rain that never came—billowed in the light breeze.

"It's hard to believe these people aren't wealthy," I whispered to Jim as I looked from right to left. Marie overheard.

"Jean-Paul did all the renovations and landscaping himself," she said, reminding me of what she'd said earlier about Jean-Paul working two jobs—stocking grocery shelves and chopping wood. He must have stocked and chopped a lot, I thought.

Jean-Paul had transformed an old mill into a fairy-tale stone cottage. Lush vines crawled over the arched wooden front doorway and around each of the leaded glass windows. As we entered the house, six-foot-three Brian ducked. Virginie, John-Paul's petite wife coiffured and immaculately dressed, flitted about the kitchen. She laughingly apologized for the size of the house, then waved us through, inviting us to explore. We shuffled from room to tiny room trying not to step on each other as we admired the way Jean-Paul had kept the original character of a mill—leaving the rock walls and wooden ceiling beams intact.

When we weren't murmuring and pointing, we were salivating over the hors d'oeuvres spread around every flat surface. There were herb-infused pâtés, savory tarts with golden crusts, miniature ravioli, tapenades of black olives and capers asking to be spread on crispy crostinis, plus piles of fresh vegetables. A beaming Virginie had prepared everything.

"Help yourself; we have no servants," shouted the handsome Jean-Paul with a grin. He stood outside and waved a tanned arm directing his guests towards the buffet tables filled with the food from the kitchen. A procession of burly men in stained aprons carried to the tables trays of grilled beef, sausages, and chicken they'd barbecued over the wood-burning pit dug at the far side of the house. We ate, we laughed and drank champagne. It was a memorable day and it wasn't over.

By early evening the voices of the guests had settled to a low murmur. I was tired and pushed back my chair ready to leave. Marie motioned me to stay seated.

"You 'ave to stay for the show," she said with a smile.

I watched as Jean-Paul walked the short distance from his table to a gravel path. We all stood. Jean-Paul held a rusty can in one hand, and a torch in the other. He turned sideways to the group, positioned the flame at arm's length, took a swig from the can, and blew a flaming orange mass from his mouth. After each successive gulp, the fiery ball grew larger and went higher. I'm sure I gasped. Jean-Paul called out to his friends to join him. One dared. He and Jean-Paul circled each other like a bull and a toreador—taking turns blowing flames in the air. The crowd clapped and cheered. Then came Act Two.

Jean-Paul smoothed back his straight dark hair, put on a worn cowboy hat, then picked up a long, thick, black leather bullwhip off a nearby table. He slowly circled the whip inches above his head several times, and then flicked his wrist. The whip cracked liked thunder. He repeated the feat several times. I may have gasped for the second time. Marie smiled.

"Jean-Paul used to do these and other cowboy tricks at an amusement park," she said, explaining the unusual entertainment.

Jean-Paul called out to the men to give it a try. The same friend who breathed fire with him tried the bullwhip. He almost tied himself up in knots and didn't manage one crack.

A tall man pushed through the crowd and walked toward Jean-Paul.

"Oh my God, it's Brian! He's going to kill himself," I shouted to Jim.

Panicked, I looked around for Tina. She'd stop him. But then I remembered she'd run up the hill to Marie's house to change her clothes after being thrown in the pool by two playful male guests.

My son-in-law Brian was in his mid-50s at the time, slim, with prematurely white hair and matching skin. He hardly fits the image of a Wild West cowboy. Amidst cheers of drunken encouragement, Jean-Paul handed Brian the hefty bullwhip. Brian carefully twirled the whip overhead a couple of times and managed to avoid hanging himself. Gasps flew from the crowd. An American tourist was surely about to choke himself to death on French soil.

Brian cracked the whip. Not once, not twice, but three times. The French villagers roared their approval. Not since 1976, when I read that a California wine surpassed a French wine in a blind taste test, have I felt prouder to be from California.

****

Snorkeling with "Orlando Bloom"

July 20, 2017

Brian surprised me one more time. It happened on the island of Porquerolles in the south of France. I was propped up on my elbows, lolling on the Mediterranean sand, squinting at the bobbing head on the distant horizon.

"It's Brian," was my daughter Tina's breezy comment. "You know he swims the shark swim every year? He just finished for the 12th time."

Tina was referring to the annual shark-infested 1.5-mile swim from Alcatraz Island to San Francisco's Aquatic Park.

I'd forgotten that her 60-year-old husband was a strong swimmer. I still felt queasy seeing him so far away from the shore.

I didn't grow up near water and never learned how to swim as a child. John Lea School gave swimming instructions in the middle of an English winter in an open-air unheated pool. Our class was bused two miles to Wilby Lido in the morning before the frost thawed. I'd line up along the concrete edge of the pool with the rest of the students—all turning various shades of blue. Our fully-clothed instructor droned on about how to breathe bubbles in the water, oblivious to the chorus of chattering teeth. We were told to throw ourselves into the frigid pool where "you will warm up once your shoulders are under the water." It was a theory the teacher declined to test out for herself. I'm not sure anyone in my group learned how to swim.

Knowing this, you can imagine how I felt when I was invited to go diving while on holiday in Porquerolles. Our French host, Marie, included my husband, Jim, and me on a scuba diving and snorkeling excursion on a neighboring island. We'd been looking forward to a lazy day.

The next morning in the dive shop at the dock, wet suits were donned, and flippers were fitted. Masks must be spat into, we're instructed—keeps them from fogging up. Once loaded with gear, we clambered aboard the 50-foot diving boat and headed for the neighboring Island of Port-Cros, a national marine sanctuary.

Neither Jim nor I had planned to scuba dive, but we did agree to go snorkeling. I'd seen films where snorkelers gently floated face down in crystal clear waters viewing a fascinating underwater world. It looked easy.

As we approached Port-Cros, the crew motioned for all aboard to jump into the swirling sea. Since the wind had picked up, the boat wouldn't be able to dock as planned. I'd imagined stepping gently into the warm Mediterranean from a sandy beach. I hadn't jumped off anything since I was 12 and that was into the shallow end of the Wilby Lido pool. I'd never worn a wet suit, flippers or a mask. Now I was being given hasty instructions on how to insert the snorkel mouthpiece.

I was primed for my first panic attack. I tripped twice as I walked to the edge of the boat. I had trouble with the snorkel. I couldn't get the hang of biting on the mouthpiece and pulling my lips over it at the same time. I was the last passenger left on the boat. The diving instructor, who was already in the water, urged me to hold the mask and jump. Adding to my mounting panic was the fact I'm not a strong swimmer. I can barely manage an awkward version of the sidestroke, which I learned at the YWCA in my late 20s. I've never been swimming in anything that didn't have sides. I was petrified. As I jumped, I knew I was about to drown.

The roiling waters engulfed me. My mask fogged up. I didn't know which way was up. I surfaced coughing and spluttering—my arms flailing. I was thrashing so wildly my husband and daughter were unable to help me. Enter the muscular, young French diving instructor, nicknamed "Orlando Bloom" by the ogling females in our party. Armed with a life preserver, he managed to wrestle me into a face-down position so I could view the underwater attractions. Swimming next to me, with one arm around my waist, the instructor gently guided me until I could propel myself. I kept a death grip on the inflatable ring.

That evening at the communal supper under the shade of an oak tree on the hotel patio, serenaded by cicadas, laughing voices recounted the day's adventure. I was teased unmercifully—charged with feigning idiocy just to have the handsome instructor put his arms around me.

Years later I shared this story with my quick-witted hiking friend, Marilee. She suggested that instead of protesting my innocence, I should have responded with a dismissive wave and a coy smile.

I wish I had thought of that.

****

What Doesn't Kill You...

"**M**om and Dad, the plans have changed," our daughter Tina alerted us. The three of us were lounging under the billowing canvas shade sails in the patio garden of the Hotel Des Medes on the gorgeous island of Porquerolles.

"Marie's brother's house in Aix-en-Provence has been rented so it's no longer available. We'll be celebrating Bastille Day in Clans instead."

After four days on the Island, Jim and I had grown accustomed to going along with the group's plans. Our French hosts, Marie and Rene Perrin, had been coming to this island, just off the south coast of France, for almost ten years. This year they had invited us, our daughter Tina and her husband,

Brian, to join them and their two children Paul and Marion, and their children's friends Audrey and Alexia. This group of ten later increased to 12 when the Perrin's longtime friends from Dijon, Anne, and Francois, ferried across from the mainland to join us.

The challenge was to get this expanded group from Porquerolles to Clans, a 13th-century medieval village high above the coastal city of Nice. The Perrins had two vehicles: a large red van that could seat six and hold most of the luggage, including six bicycles, as well as a Peugeot that could seat five. Jim and I offered to ride the train. This was not a sacrifice on my part. I am a terrible passenger, scared witless by the fast French drivers. Marie arranged for a friend to meet us in Nice and drive us to Clans.

A small car with a smiling woman behind the wheel beckoned to us as we stood outside the Nice station. As Jim and I clambered into the car of Marie's friend, Anne, I asked how she had identified us. "It was easy, " she said with a smile, "Marie said Jim looked like a cross between a lumberjack and Santa Claus." Jim liked the comparison.

We agreed to Anne's invitation for a short tour of the city's downtown.

"Nice," Anne informed us in perfect English, "is part of the region known in France as the Cote d'Azur, which means the deep blue coast. English-speaking people incorrectly refer to the area as the

French Riviera. In France we refer to the Italian side as the Riviera."

Anne drove along the coastal road adjacent to the Promendade des Anglais[1], the pedestrian walk that traces the shores of the sparkling Mediterranean. We traveled slowly enough to enjoy the view of sailboats, luxury yachts, and sunbathers lounging in iconic blue deck chairs—protection from the rocky beach.

"There," Anne pointed, waving her arm, "is the famous Hotel Negresco."

We turned our heads towards an immense domed building that looked like a palace. Built in 1912 by Henri Negresco, it is now a combination museum-hotel. An eye-catching ten-foot statue of Miles Davis welcomes visitors at the front entrance—a testament to the affection the French have for Black entertainers in general, and American Jazz in particular.

Anne interspersed the history of Nice with stories of her friendship with Marie. Both she and Marie were born and raised in Senegal, a former French colony in West Africa. Their fathers were professionals, and the families grew up in relative luxury—accustomed to servants. Anne's remark about servants triggered my memory of a

---

[1] *It was unimaginable to us at that time that a few years later the Promendade des Anglais would become the scene of a horrific terrorist attack.*

conversation with Marie's mother, Nora. I had expressed admiration for raising five children. She replied that had she not lived in Senegal, her family would have been smaller.

As we sped along, rows of multi-story resort condominiums gave way to small clusters of whitewashed houses that were in turn replaced by rocky hills and deep ravines.

Jim told me later that during all his years of mountain road construction, he had never before seen what we saw that day: rock ledges overhanging the road. Mercifully, there was chain link netting designed to catch any falling boulders.

In some places the road would narrow into a single lane that would disappear around a blind curve.

"What happens," I squeaked from the back seat, "when another car comes in the opposite direction."

"Oh," Anne replied airily, "one of us backs up."

We're not that far from Monaco. Isn't this where Princess Grace hurtled off a French Riviera cliff?

With that happy thought, I gripped the edge of my seat even tighter. I was glad I was seated in the back and could hide my fear behind a permanent fake smile. Occasionally, I would throw a sneer towards the back of Jim's head wondering how he could chatter on so merrily about the wonderful scenery in the face of our impending death drop.

We arrived in Clans in one piece. I can't say the drive was worth it, but it was close. Out of the car, with two feet firmly planted on solid ground, I could appreciate the magnificent panoramic view of the granite mountains, and the deep, lush green ravines.

As we walked up the steep, narrow path, Tina was working her way down the hill to greet us.

"Can you believe this place?" she cooed. We were surrounded by beauty. We climbed the rock steps to the cobblestone streets admiring the houses with their wrought-iron window boxes filled with scarlet blooms hanging in front of dark-stained shutters. Terracotta planters stood sentry by front doors. Sweet-faced sunflowers followed the fading light. Despite our excited chatter, there was a stillness and serenity about the village. Marie had told us there were only 300 people living in Clans—and no tourists. Visitors were either relatives or close friends.

In our excitement, we almost forgot to celebrate the birthdays of Jim and our son-in-law, Brian. Glasses of Kier Royale were passed through the low kitchen window to the adults seated outside on wooden benches next to Anne's sister Mimi's house. Platters of delicacies quickly followed. A chorus of French and English voices singing "Happy Birthday," ricocheted off the stone houses.

"My sister Mimi has made chili in honor of our American guests," announced Anne. I wasn't aware that chili was a particularly American dish, but the sentiment was lovely. The meal was delicious, ending with the usual array of cheese.

"Before we go to the village Bastille Day[2] celebration, we must go on a special walk tonight," Marie said between sips of our host's treasured Bordeaux.

We were barely able to move after supper, but Jim and I gamely joined the rest of the group on the walk that Marie had suggested. It was dark by the time we reached the village square filled with celebrators.

"Follow me," called out Marie, "and stay to the left near the rock face."

Except for the occasional spark from a firefly, the night was pitch black. I held Jim's hand. I'm not a good judge of distance but I'm sure we walked a couple of miles. The teenagers in the group were enjoying themselves. I could hear them up ahead, laughing. Jim and I caught up with them. We'd apparently reached the end of the walk. I was tired and ready for bed, and we still had to walk back.

On our return we were greeted by our host, Anne. She had graciously given up her bedroom to Jim and me.

"My father was born and raised in this house," she explained as we followed her up the uneven stone steps to the small weather-beaten front door a few

---

2. Bastille Day is a national holiday commemorating the storming of the Bastille prison in Paris, which marked the beginning of the French Revolution. Celebrations are similar to the 4th of July festivities in the U.S., culminating in spectacular firework displays.

feet across from Mimi's house. "Later he purchased three houses here in Clans. This house for me, the one across the street for Mimi, and another in the village for our brother. You will sleep here," she said opening another wooden door leading into a small, low-ceilinged room. Later, I tumbled into bed—drifting off to the sound of water trickling from the wall fountain outside the window.

Next morning before everyone gathered for breakfast, I suggested to Jim that we retrace our walk from the night before. I wanted to see the area in the daylight. After passing the village square we followed the only narrow path leading away from the town. Once on the road, I realized that if more than four people had walked abreast on the trail we took in total darkness, one would have fallen into an abyss. I asked Jim if it was too early for wine

****

Brooklyn to Bodega Bay

If you were driving across America between August and October in 2015, you might have seen a smiling Dutchman pedaling furiously with a cigar behind his right ear and a Snickers bar in his left hand. It's possible the neck of a German beer peeked from a corner of his handlebar bag. The rider was my friend, Wisse.

I first met Wisse and his lovely wife, Franka during one of our visits to Vignieu. Eight of us, known in the town as "The Americans," were staying with Marie and Renee, Wisse's niece and her husband.

A decade later Wisse is sitting in my kitchen in California. He's lean and tanned and happy. Two days before he'd completed a solo cycling marathon—Brooklyn to Bodega Bay—biking 2,200 of the 3,000 miles in 33 days—driven a few hundred miles by a visiting Dutch friend.

Back in the '70's, Wisse had worked in the U.S. and planned to return. It took him a few years. Judging from his Facebook posts, the wait was worth it. Wisse wrote eloquently about America's vast and lush landscape—the beautiful forests, lakes, creeks, and rivers. He marveled at Yellowstone's waterfalls and geysers. He'd never seen any expanse of water to compare with the Missouri and Mississippi rivers, "As beautiful as I've ever seen," his mother would have said.

Wisse appreciated the clean highways and thought it a novelty many were maintained by private sponsors. Old railroad tracks transformed into biking and walking lanes were ingenious. There weren't many scooters or mopeds, he lamented, but no shortage of tattooed motorcyclists—all resembling Hulk Hogan, riding without helmets on huge bikes.

But it wasn't just the size and beauty of America that captured Wisse. A car enthusiast, he noticed how lovingly Americans restored classic Mustangs and Corvettes. He wondered why Americans didn't treat their bodies with as much care.

The Dutchman must be 6'4" and could only eat half the food he was served. He took photographs of his meals to amaze his friends in Holland. He drank his first good cup of coffee in Ohio and, surprise, it was brewed in a Douwe Egberts Dutch coffee machine. Coffee refills bemused him: "You can never finish your coffee in the United States."

On a quiet road in Pennsylvania Wisse stopped to talk to an Amish farmer. There were no classic cars, just the clip-clop of passing horse-drawn buggies. Wisse was intrigued with the Amish life, as most are—living without electricity, cars, and phones. He learned the Amish carve ice blocks from the river to preserve food. And, he just had to note: "They are not fat."

I'm sure Wisse's blue eyes twinkled whenever he wrote about the size of Americans and their food portions. After all, these health bulletins came from a man whose daily routine included smoking cigars, drinking beer and eating Snickers bars.

Motels received a thumbs up. They had everything and were cheap, too. During one stop Wisse accidentally did someone else's laundry. "An hour later I did my own."

Convenience stores were, well, convenient. Wisse could replenish essential supplies—cigars, Snickers, Coke, and beer. The state of Utah was the exception. Wisse was astounded, and more than a little put out that a restaurant in Salt Lake City didn't serve beer. "Strange, to put it politely."

There were a few scares. Wisse was almost hit by a truck in New Jersey, and tunnels on the Nevada interstate were nerve-racking. He'd like to forget the Devils Elbow in Pennsylvania. The road was stony, slippery and so steep he rode halfway up in the lowest gear, then careened downhill. He was relieved he was riding a "handmade, reinforced steel Rohloff Naaf equipped with the Rolls Royce of cycle gears." The only problem he had with his bike was a flat tire caused by a thistle he picked up in Petaluma, California.

The people he met were mostly friendly. In the town of Strawberry near Lake Tahoe, when Wisse was wet and frozen following an icy rain, a couple invited him, a stranger, into their home to spend the night.

One notable exception to this goodwill happened when Wisse began his journey from Brooklyn. Two bridges on his route were blocked, another was open, but closed to cyclists. Wisse took it anyway. The police were waiting on the other side. They gave Wisse a New York greeting: "We don't (expletive) care where you come from! Next time we'll arrest you."

Wisse's Facebook page shows he's already planning his next adventure—biking the trail from the Spanish-French border to the city of Santiago de Compostela, a journey of 1,400 miles from his home in Holland.

I wished him well and asked if he had any final words about his trip across America. He did:

"America is the best country in the world and can never be conquered. "

I know those blue eyes were twinkling.

Postscript: Wisse accomplished his second marathon bike ride from his home near Amsterdam to the city of Santiago de Compostela—cycling almost 1,400 miles in 26 days. "It was a great, beautiful, heavy, interesting trip," he wrote on Facebook. "There was a tsunami of pilgrims."

This royal wedding portrait features Prince Harry and Duchess Meghan with their parents, his grandparents and the pageboys and bridesmaids.(Photo: Alexi Lubomirski, Kensington Palace)

RACIAL PROFILES

*Race is not an easy subject for me. I don't belong to one, but two races. I'm not hyper-sensitive to racial differences, but I'm also not immune to them as evidenced by the following four stories: "**The Royal Box**," a glimpse of the challenges of a biracial American actress before she became a British duchess; "**Loving versus Virginia**," the title of an*

157

*historic court case that struck down the ban on interracial marriage in America, and one that had personal ramifications; "**Golly**," the name of a black rag doll that evoked fond memories in some and hurtful ones in others, and "**The Celebration**," honoring the life of Martin Luther King Jr. in a predominately white, conservative community.*

The Royal Box

May 18, 2018, The Union

I had never watched the TV law drama, *Suits*, so had no idea who Meghan Markle is. I, and the world, now knows she is the young woman who, on May 19, 2018, married Henry Charles Albert David Mountbatten-Windsor, aka Prince Harry, sixth in line to the throne of the United Kingdom. What made this union more newsworthy than the marriage of a British prince would be, is that Ms. Markle is an American, an actress, a divorcée, and happens to be biracial—one Black parent and one Caucasian one—like me.

In an interview she gave to *Elle Magazine* in 2015, a year before she met Prince Harry, Ms. Markle talks candidly about growing up biracial in a non-diverse section of Los Angeles. The article: *Meghan Markle: I'm More than An 'Other'* is worth a read.

The *Elle* article begins with "What are you?" That is a question often asked of those whose race is indiscernible. Meghan plays coy. She answers to a "who" rather than a "what."

"I'm an actress, a writer, the Editor-in-Chief of my lifestyle brand 'The Tig', a pretty good cook, and a firm believer in handwritten notes." You would think that laundry list would suffice. Instead, there's always the follow-up: "Right, but what are you? Where are your parents from?" Meghan gives up. "I'm half black and half white."

I've never been asked "what are you?" because unlike Ms. Markle, I look biracial. But I've been asked where I was from because I have the remnants of a British accent. When I respond that I was born and raised in England, the response is often a squinty look followed by a suspicious, "You don't look English." The dark curly hair and brown skin confuses them. I've heard more than one American express dismay after returning from a trip to London where they discovered the place was teaming with "foreigners"—dark-skinned people in other words. It's not only Americans who find swarthy faces incongruent with British accents. I have family and friends in England who've had difficulty adjusting to a modern Britain that is evolving from a homogenous society to a multi-racial one.

The magazine photographs of Ms. Markle show her coloring to be similar to that of my daughter, Tina, an accomplished environmental attorney. Like Meghan, there's nothing about Tina's appearance that would identify her as having African ancestry.

In junior high school she was cursed for being "Mexican" by Caucasian girls and insulted for being "white" by Latinas. When she casually told me this one evening, I was furious. But my daughter was amused at being racially undefinable. She found it exotic.

But Tina did not find amusing or exotic happened when she was in high school. The mother of her friend, who happened to be Caucasian, asked Tina, "Why would you tell people you are part black when nobody would know?" The woman was not malicious; she was mystified. She was proclaiming loud and clear that to be part African-American was something to be ashamed of—something to hide if you could.

I was relieved these insensitive episodes didn't upset Tina. I grew up in an all-white Irish family in an all-white community in England. When kids called out cruel names to me, I was confused and hurt. I didn't feel different from them. I was surprised each time a person identified me as "colored." I've often read where single-race people think mixed-race children are doomed to grow up confused and conflicted. They may when ridiculed for being different, or forced into a racial category that denies any part of who they are. We're not born confused or conflicted.

In the *Elle* article Meghan explains that when completing a mandatory census in the seventh grade, she was faced with selecting an ethnicity box that included four choices: Caucasian, Black, Hispanic or Asian. Because she looked white, her teacher advised her to check the white box. Meghan couldn't do that—doing so would deny the other parent. She put down her pen. She wasn't being rebellious. Rather, she felt sad. When she relayed the story to her father, he told her something that she has never forgotten.

Meghan's father told his daughter that if the situation happened again, she should draw her own box. Judging from the *Elle* article, Meghan Markle has done just that.

I hope that Meghan's example will inspire "others" in Great Britain and America to do the same.

****

"Loving Versus Virginia"

November 25, 2016

On my long list of films to see is the movie, "Loving." The title is both subject and surname. Richard and Mildred Loving, an interracial couple—he Caucasian, she African-American and Native American—struggle for nine years to overturn Virginia's miscegenation law. The time was

1958. Little did I know that my first marriage, in 1963, violated that same law.

Frank was an 18-year-old Caucasian airman, born in Virginia and stationed near my hometown in England's East Midlands. I was British, biracial, and 17 years old when we met in 1962. Our courtship was a rocky one for reasons unrelated to race. I was insecure and easily intimidated. Frank was opinionated and tactless. I thought it was because he wasn't British.

In the spring of 1962 I unintentionally joined "the pudding club." I'd failed to follow my Irish mother's birth control advice: "Keep your hand on your ha'penny 'till you get your toffee."

"We'll get married," Frank announced. I wasn't thrilled with the idea, but it was better than being an unmarried mother. Frank gave me an engagement ring with a single diamond in the shape of a heart to show he was serious. I removed the ring whenever I put my hands in water, and one day it slipped from the soapy ledge above the sink and swirled down the drain. It was an omen.

Frank needed his mother's permission to marry so the mandatory counseling meeting with the military chaplain doubled as a report to Frank's mother, Alzona, in Virginia. She refused to give her consent. Frank learned the chaplain had told her I looked part black. I realized that squinty look the chaplain gave me hadn't been a figment of my imagination. Frank ranted over the phone at his mother and I wrote pleading for her consent. It was only after seeing the photograph of our baby boy that she relented.

I knew there were serious problems between blacks and whites in America. I was stunned to see the violent clashes between the races on television. To see the signs designating "white" or "colored" in restaurant windows, above water fountains, on bathroom doors and in other public places, made my heart ache for all the African Americans who were demeaned by this attitude. And yet, Frank and I never discussed race. I hadn't a clue there were 24 states that banned interracial marriage. Two years later in 1965, and now a family of four, we left England for Frank's next assignment in New Mexico. We decided to visit Alzona in Virginia.

Frank's mother opened the door of her brick house in Roanoke, Virginia and greeted each of us with a warm hug. She lifted both children on her lap calling them "doll babies," and kissed them, insisting they give her lots of "sugar" in return.

I soon discovered that Frank and his mother had more than looks in common. Alone with Alzona one evening, out of the blue she said, "I'm surprised you're so big. Ivan always had tiny girlfriends." She called my husband by his middle name because she didn't want to be reminded of "her louse of an ex-husband," who was named Frank.

My mouth dropped open after hearing Alzona's rude comment. I was hardly the size of Tessie

O'Shea—a large singer my mother used as a reference for overweight people. But even if I were—who says such a thing to someone's face? Alzona also had an earthy sense of humor. I was horrified when she told me a dirty joke. I managed to squeak out a tight smile and hoped it didn't look like a grimace.

Alzona followed up these startling conversations with: "Would you like some tea, honey?" I was dying for a cuppa. My mother-in-law returned from the kitchen with a tall glass filled with orange-colored liquid and ice cubes. I didn't want to be rude, *unlike some people*, so I drank as much as I could. I had swallowed my first—and my last—glass of iced tea.

We visited Alzona's three sisters who, thank goodness, did not inherit the tactless gene. They hugged and kissed me and the children and presented us with belated wedding presents and toys for the children. Our visit was turning out to be a lot more pleasant than I'd expected until one evening. As Frank drove his mother, me and the children home from a day of sightseeing he pointed to a small brick house across from his mother's place saying he'd like to buy it for his family.

"You know you can't live here, Ivan," Alzona said. I was stunned. I had no idea that Virginia was one of the 24 states that banned interracial marriage.

Frank was furious. We packed and left that night leaving behind the wedding gifts and the children's presents. Everyone, except Frank, cried as we left

Alzona's house. We had never planned to live in Virginia, and, unlike the couple in the movie, Frank and I didn't have to wait for the 1967 Supreme Court decision, "Loving vs Virginia," to live together. We were headed for New Mexico, one of 18 states that had already repealed the ban on interracial marriage.

****

Golly

March 1, 2018

One of the last places I expected to see knick-knacks from the Jim Crow era was in a store set back on a winding two-lane road out of Auburn, California. Those items peered at me from inside a massive glass-fronted, mirrored cabinet.

On display was a rack of five spice jars: containers for salt, pepper, and vinegar, and large "Mammy" cookie jars. All had coal black faces with thick bright red lips and enlarged whites of their eyes— demeaning caricatures of Africans and African Americans.

I asked "Sally," the store owner, if I could take a photograph of the collection, letting her know that I was a writer. She agreed and surprised me by saying she was glad I had stopped in. She asked if I had an opinion about the display. Her son, she said, got upset when he saw it.

"He told me I should remove them, that the items were insulting to African Americans and represent an ugly period in America. I said that I had been conflicted, but when I questioned my customers, none was offended. They considered them Americana—representations of American history.

"My son asked, 'what color skin did these customers have?'

Sally lowered her eyes.

"White, I answered."

Then she gave me a concerned look and asked, "How did you feel when you saw them?"

I told her I was startled and had to turn away. They had brought back a painful memory from my childhood in England.

"Have you heard of a gollywog?" I asked Sally. She shook her head. I told her this personal story.

A gollywog is a black rag doll, a caricature of an American minstrel, I explained. This image was the trademark of the Robertson Company, the most popular jam maker in England in the 1950s. Golly, as he was known, grinned on the label of the jam pot that sat on the table in our house every Sunday at teatime. One of my siblings would point to the jar, then point to me, and all the kids would giggle. I had frizzy black hair and was the only brown face at a table of Irish faces. I'd cry, which guaranteed the teasing would continue.

I went on to tell Sally that I'd read in *The Atlantic* about a Jim Crow Museum housed at the Ferris State

University in Michigan. For four decades its founder, Dr. David Pilgrim, had collected racist artifacts— signs, pictures, and knick-knacks—like the ones in her shop—that belittle Africans and their American descendants. He's also created a traveling exhibit that includes objects that subjugate women, gays, Jewish Americans, Native Americans, Mexican Americans, Asian Americans, and poor whites. Dr. Pilgrim explains that he uses "objects of intolerance to teach tolerance and promote social justice."

I told Sally, that if the price were right, I'd purchase the collection and donate it to the Ferris Museum. She said she'd contact the out-of-town owner.

On my ride home I remembered how surprised I was to read that Dr. Pilgrim's traveling exhibit included poor whites as a group subject to ridicule. Then I recalled when an editor pointed out a stereotype. She was upset by my memoir's mention of "... toothless mountain men, armed with shotguns ...accompanied by dueling banjos," referencing the film classic, *Deliverance*. She grew up in Georgia where the movie was made. Her community was appalled by the derogatory stereotyping of white southerners of that region. That thought never occurred to me. I revised the section.

I read that the Robertson Company also made a change. After 90 years, it finally removed their golliwog logo in 2002.

The golliwog is off the jam jars but not the front pages. A 2013 article in BBC News reported on responses to a shop in Brighton, England selling drink mats depicting Golliwog illustrations. One 72-year-old woman thought there was "...no harm in them. They are nostalgic..."

A Black History Group member told of his experience. In the 1960s he'd walked around not knowing someone had stuck a Robertson golliwog label on his back. "It was used to tease us, and it was used as a racist term."

The *Telegraph online* reported a few years ago that Carol Thatcher, daughter of the late former British Prime Minister Margaret Thatcher, made what she called a "silly joke." She referred to the French tennis play Jo-Wilfried Tsonga—who looks like a young Mohammed Ali—as looking like a golliwog. Ms. Thatcher stated she had no idea she was being offensive, and was merely comparing Tsonga to the doll she had as a child. She was eligible for the 'clueless' award.

Australia has also had its Golly moments. An outcry broke out when a shop, Terry White Chemists—a pharmacy—displayed a sign inviting shoppers to, "Experience a White Christmas," referring to the name of the Chemist. Underneath the sign were nine golliwog dolls.

I laughed out loud when I read this. I believed the shop manager when he said he hadn't made a connection between the dolls and the sign. Terry

White Chemists banned the sale of the gollywogs. I hope they received the 'clued-in' award.

When I visited Sally's store the following week, I learned the owner wanted the ridiculous price of a thousand dollars for the offensive ceramics.

Sally had already removed the collection from the cabinet. They had been packed up and put out of sight in a back room.

****

A Celebration

January 21, 2018

I arrived half an hour early determined to find a parking space close to the General Gomez Arts and Event Center where the Martin Luther King Jr. celebration was being held.

With time to spare, I crossed the street to The Healthy Habit restaurant. It was early and the place was empty. When the waitress emerged from a back area, I ordered a latte. She looked at me with an expression that said, "Do we look like Starbucks?"

Only regular coffee was available—prepared upon request.

"We have golden milk," she offered with a pleasant smile.

"Sounds lovely," I said and forked over five dollars.

Minutes later, I was served a frothy mustard-colored concoction in a porcelain bowl that could double as a baby bathtub. The drink was delicious.

While nursing my beverage, I stared out of the window into two hypnotic emerald eyes. They were peering at me from the Monkey Cat Restaurant sign on the ivy-covered wall kitty-corner to the café.

I dawdled for as long as I thought respectable, then walked a couple of blocks down Lincoln Way to the Golden Swan jewelry store, one of my favorite places to browse. I'd read in the *Auburn Journal* the store had been robbed two days earlier. Ben Asgarzadeh, the co-owner, was outside. Several boxes filled with shattered glass were lined up by the curb. The broken window had been replaced. I told Ben how sorry my husband, Jim, and I were to read about this latest robbery. He looked sad.

"It's the third time," he said shaking his head. I repeated my condolences, turned and walked back to the event center.

By the time the first speaker took the microphone, the Gomez center was packed. Those who couldn't find a seat were either sitting or standing in the aisles. I was pleased to see a couple of familiar faces. There was Rosalie Wohlfromm, activist and writer, and Leo, a hiking group friend. I recognized a few other faces: Placer County Supervisor Jennifer Montgomery, smiling and energized as usual wearing what looked like an early Easter bonnet. John Bowman, a freelance editor and writer leaned across a seat to shake my hand. I recognized Leslye Janusz, a well-known community activist, and one of the speakers. Leslye surprised me when she announced that 12 people attended the first King celebration, held 34 years ago. Leslie was one of them.

The morning's program was advertised as "a multicultural and multigenerational program of music, poetry and community voices." It was all of that, and more.

A young woman stood and identified herself as an illegal immigrant, brought to the United States as a child. She's one of the hundreds of thousands who could be deported as early as March if Congress doesn't act to renew the Deferred Action for Childhood Arrivals (DACA), or agree to something more permanent. I managed to stop from getting teary by looking away every few seconds.

Another participant stepped forward to tell his story. He'd lived with his grandfather, a stroke victim, for the first seven years of his life. The speaker told the story of when he was a young boy, playing on the floor beside his grandfather's recliner. The elderly man, he said, stood and blurted out "Go to Stanford." The boy, of course, didn't know what a Stanford was. Fast forward and the speaker is a senior in high school preparing to apply to a college. When the school counselor handed him an application to a state college, his grandfather's words popped into his head. "I want to apply to Stanford," he said. The counselor responded that the school only has so many Stanford applications, and they were going to the top students. The speaker said he gave the state college application back. When he got home he contacted Stanford directly.

He did get accepted, and graduated. He told the gathering, "Tell your children and grandchildren what they can do, not what they cannot," the speaker concluded. "You may not think your kids are listening, but they are."

After almost three hours, the program drew to a close. Stan Padilla, an acquaintance, artist, educator, and social activist, gave inspirational closing remarks and encouraged the audience to join the march to the town center's fire pit.

On the drive home I thought about how moved I was by all the speakers—each performing a service to the community—an encouragement to the audience to do the same.

The morning's program, recognizing the life and legacy of Martin Luther King, brought together our multicultural community, an occurrence I rarely see.

In today's climate of political and social division this was also something to celebrate.

಄಄

Poppa's House

THE LAST HOUSE BEFORE SPAIN

The parents of my mother-in-law, Betty, were French Basque. Betty couldn't speak English when she started school in California, and the kids referred to her as a "french fry." The name sounded almost cute to me—someone who'd been ridiculed for the color of my skin. But any name that serves to separate is cruel.

Betty's mother, Marie, died when Betty was 16. Her father, John Maitia, affectionately known as "Poppa," was alive and well when I arrived in California from England in the winter of 1970.

Poppa was one of many who fled from Europe to America during World War I. Like thousands from the Basque region in the Pyrenees, John Maitia was a sheepherder, and plied his trade in California for decades.

*The stories that follow describe the efforts of my husband, Jim, and me to find Poppa's birthplace: "**Be Careful What You Wish For**," "**Eye of the Beholder**," "**Trip to Biarittz**," and "**The Last House**."*

Our adventure was almost over before it began.

Be Careful What You Wish For

You'd think being born in England, a mere 20-mile leap across the English Channel to France, that I would've been a frequent visitor to the Continent. I wasn't. I waited until I immigrated to America. Now I travel thousands of miles to see sights that I could've seen on a day trip.

One bright July morning, my husband, Jim, and I are riding a train on our way to San Francisco to catch an evening flight to Paris. Halfway to

Emeryville, a passenger seated behind us whispered to the back of our heads:

"An airplane has crash-landed at the San Francisco airport."

I gasped. Voices rose as other passengers shared the terrible news.

At the Emeryville Station, we interrupted our shuttle driver talking to his dispatcher.

"The off-ramps to the airport are closed," he told us. "What do you want to do?"

We asked to be dropped off at any hotel close to the airport. Televisions in the hotel lounge blasted news of the crash. Asiana Airline flight 214 from Seoul, South Korea, had crashed.

After repeated calls to our airline, a British voice assured us the airport had reopened. Our flight was scheduled to leave that evening.

At the airport, media people were running around with cameras on their shoulders thrusting microphones in the faces of anyone who looked Asian.

Our flight was delayed for two hours—a short wait considering a plane had crashed. We had no idea what had happened to the passengers and crew.

On board the packed plane, waiting for take-off, I closed my eyes and held my breath—my usual position when flying. The plane didn't move.

A crackling voice came over the intercom.

"Ladies and gentlemen we're experiencing a slight delay. We have a fuel leak, possibly from overfueling. We'll be on our way as soon as possible. Thank you for your patience."

I gave my husband a "save me" look, but he was staring out the window.

"There. Can you see it?" he said, pointing to the wing.

I couldn't see a thing. Jim repeated the directions. Finally, I see the pool of liquid on the tarmac.

"It's probably the emergency fuel dump valve," Jim said, drawing on his past experience as a fuel systems mechanic in the Air Force. "It's not going to be an easy fix."

Emergency vehicles and personnel surrounded the plane. Bags of white powder were poured around the expanding puddle.

A flight attendant served us a glass of water and a small carton of something I couldn't identify. My watch showed 1:30 a.m. We'd been on the plane for four hours.

I walked to the front of the aircraft. A small group had gathered around several flight attendants who'd opened the boarding door to let in air. Several people demanded to be let off. The captain appealed for patience explaining the luggage would have to be located for anyone that leaves the plane, causing further delays.

The problem was finally fixed. We were ready to take off. The aircraft moved. Wing flaps down; engines revved up. I held my breath and again closed my eyes. I told myself that I was probably the oldest person on the plane—that I'd had a pretty good life. That there were worse ways to leave this earth, although I couldn't think of any at that moment.

A passenger behind us screamed, "It's leaking again!"

The plane slowed to a stop. I opened my eyes. Fuel was streaming from the same wing. More intercom apologies and assurances—more emergency vehicles and personnel.

I can't believe this is happening. Why don't they let us off?

It is now 4:30 a.m. The intercom crackled again. We would be towed back to the boarding gate. We'd been in this aluminum tube for seven hours. Our flight was re-scheduled for 3:30 p.m.—11 hours from then.

Later, in the boarding queue, passengers were asking the same questions: "Why didn't they let us off as soon as they discovered the first leak? We could have been burned alive. Does anyone know what was in that pudding they served us?"

We boarded again, but three hours later than scheduled. The plane taxied and made a slow wide turn preparing for takeoff. This time my eyes were open.

The wreckage of Flight 214 lay like a gigantic wounded gooney bird on an adjacent runway. The landing gear and tail were sheared off. There were two charred, gaping holes in the fuselage. Deflated escape chutes sagged from the emergency exits.

We'd learn the pilot had come in too low and too slow. He hit the rock seawall when he tried to abort the landing.

As our plane climbed into the clouds I remembered what I'd casually mentioned to friends:

"I hope I have something interesting to write about our vacation."

****

Eye of the Beholder

One thing led to another after our Virgin Airline's flight from San Francisco to London was delayed for 24 hours due to an emergency. We missed our connecting British Airways' flight to Bordeaux, France and forfeited a one-night hotel stay in that city, along with the next day's train ticket to Bayonne.

When we'd arrived at London's Heathrow, we went straight to Virgin's ticket counter. We knew they would fix things.

The airline staff all but said, too bad, so sad. Our connecting flight to Bordeaux was with another airline, they told us. We trundled off to the British Airways' counter.

"Our airline," responded a smug employee, "had no delays. We're not responsible."

So here we were stuck in Heathrow Airport after spending ten hours flying with our knees around our ears, and no help or sympathy from anyone.

"I'll call Tina," I told my husband as I tried not to cry. "She'll know what to do."

First I had to activate our European cell phone. My credit card was rejected three times before I managed to wrestle a cellphone SIM card out of a kiosk.

Back in California, our daughter, Tina, oozed sympathy. I sniffled; a few tears squeaked out.

"Let me see what I can do," she said in her best lawyer voice.

Jim had found a place to sit, for a price, and was sipping a Guinness while we waited for Tina to call back. I fumbled the phone open.

"Here goes Mother," Tina said. "I've done a thorough Internet search, and this is the only way you will get from London to France tonight. I have you and dad booked on the Eurostar, the train that goes under the English Channel. You need to get to St. Pancras International Railway Station. You'll pick up your Eurostar tickets from a kiosk at the station.

Oh no, another kiosk.

Here are the confirmation numbers." I scribbled them on a beer napkin.

"Eurostar will take you to a place called Lille—it's north of Paris. (Our destination was Bayonne in the south on the Spanish border). I've reserved a one-night stay at the Why Hotel in Lille. Don't ask why it's called The Why. (I smiled for the first time in days). The next morning you'll pick up your tickets at the Lille Station, and these will get you to Paris' Gare Du Nord. You'll need to take a taxi to the other station in Paris—the Montparnasse—which will take you to Bayonne."

I thanked Tina and told her she was wonderful. Jim gulped the last of his beer, and we headed to St. Pancras.

For some time I'd wanted to take the Channel Tunnel, a 35-mile train line under the English Channel, also known as the Chunnel. I remember reading about the Chunnel when it opened in 1994. What an engineering feat. A tunnel under the roiling waters of the English Channel. I'd crossed the Channel on a ferry when I was 18, and pregnant. Everyone on board was seasick. I would've appreciated a tunnel even if it is a scary 250 feet under the sea.

The Hotel Why in Lille was modern and spotless. The next morning, after oversleeping and missing the free breakfast, we headed for the station where I managed to extract our tickets from the kiosk. Six hours and one station change later, we were in Bayonne.

We'd been here before. Four years ago, on our way to visit friends in northern France, Jim and I detoured south to Bayonne to find the birthplace of my husband's Basque grandfather. We were unlucky then, and returned to try again.

"Wouldn't it be nice," I'd told my husband en route from the Bayonne station to the hotel, "if they gave us the same room at the Le Grand."

A heat wave had engulfed Europe and the hotel receptionist apologized for not having a room with air conditioning. We must have looked dejected because he checked again and announced that he did have an air conditioned room after all.

"Does it overlook the church?" I'd asked. To his credit, he didn't sneer, but checked again, smiled, and said it did.

We maneuvered our suitcases into the wrought-iron elevator, squeezed in, and were hoisted up to the third floor. As we trudged along the corridor, I recognized the pictures on the wall and remembered the bump in the floor.

We had our same room.

Once inside I rushed to repeat that first magical experience of opening the casement window and hearing the church bells. What I saw was a giant tower crane.

Jim was standing behind me.

"Wow," he'd said, and I turned to see a smile on his face. "That's a Potain Crane, just like the one I ran on the construction of The Holiday Inn years ago."

****

Trip to Biarittz

Posted speed limits serve as suggestions to my husband, and French drivers in Bayonne seemed to agree. They appear to be in training for Le Mans.

Jim is comfortable driving in France because, he told me, the French, unlike the British, drive on the *right* side of the road. Still he needed time to get used to the rental car.

"Please take me back to the hotel," I pleaded after the fifth near miss with cars entering and exiting roundabouts.

"I know I'm making you nervous. I can shop while you drive around," I offered.

I didn't have to ask twice.

Jim wasn't gone long. I was lolling in a sidewalk café up the hill from the hotel when he found me.

"You have to come with me," he said, looking happier than when he'd dropped me off. "I drove to Biarittz; it's not that far."

Biarittz was not our intended destination. We were in France to find the town of Esterencuby, the birthplace of my husband's French Basque grandfather. This was the second time we'd travelled to this region. We had failed to find Poppa's house on the earlier trip.

I wasn't prepared for the beauty of Biarittz. It hit me when we reached the top of a hill in the town's center. Jim told me I gasped.

Before us stretched the brilliant turquoise waters of the Bay of Biscay, a golden beach, and tall jagged rocks rising from the sea. I wished I'd been with Jim earlier when he had seen the Bay for the first time.

After several spins around the town we found a place to park then joined the throngs as they strolled along the promenade. There were people everywhere. They crowded the sidewalks as they window shopped or sat cheek to cheek on park benches. While I admired the lush vegetation and brilliantly-colored blooming hydrangea bushes that edged the streets, Jim squinted against the sun to see the rock formations. How could we have missed this place during our earlier trip?

We'd learn later this coastal city is one of the most popular vacation spots in the world. As we walked, Jim pointed to an imposing white statue mounted on an immense rock tunnel. To reach the tunnel we crossed an iron footbridge built on rocks jutting above the sea. The bridge was built by Gustav Eiffel, the builder of the Eiffel Tower.

Legend has it that whalers put up the statue. As we approached the sculpture we could see it portrayed the Virgin Mary and Christ Child. A bright light is said to glow from the rock, warning sailors away from the shoreline.

On our way back to the car I regretted that we hadn't done our homework and made time to visit the majestic seafront Hotel du Palais, a palace built by Empress Eugenie, wife of Napoleon III.

I took my last look at the Bay before climbing into the car.

"I thought the French went topless?" I asked Jim as I scanned the crowded beach.

"Some do," he answered with the hint of a smile.

And I'd thought he was fascinated by the rock formations.

On the road back to Bayonne, Jim suggested having dinner at the restaurant on the river. He was referring to the "Talaia," a boat anchored on the Adour River.

During our first visit to Bayonne, we'd sauntered past this restaurant several times, but it had always been closed. At that time we were not accustomed to the French meal schedule. Dinner was usually served an hour before our bedtime. That night we managed to stay awake; the meal at the Talaia was worth it.

Even though it was dark by the time we finished our meal, we were comfortable strolling across the pedestrian bridges and along the now-familiar river banks. As we walked back to the hotel Jim reminded me of something.

"Did you know Bayonne is at the confluence of two rivers: the Nive and the Adour? It's like

Sacramento with the American and Sacramento Rivers."

I shook my head. I'd forgotten that connection.

One more reason to love this place.

Our stay in Bayonne was shortened from four nights to three due to the earlier travel disruptions. Now we only had one more full day to finish our search.

The next morning, armed with maps, photographs, and a family tree diagram, we set off to find the home of Jim's grandfather, John Maitia. But first, we had to learn how to pronounce Esterencuby.

****

The Last House Before Spain

Rested and ready to go, we stopped on the way out of the Bayonne hotel to ask the hotel clerk for directions. We spread our map across the counter and explained we were searching for the town where Jim's grandfather, affectionately called "Poppa," was born. We had been unable to find Esterencuby on the map.

When Jim spoke the name of the town, the clerk gave us a blank look. Jim and I tried different pronunciations. After our third attempt, the clerk smiled. "Ahh Estersoobee." He looked at the map and pointed to the town of St. Jean Pied De Port, apparently the closest town to Esterencuby.

"Do we know exactly where we're going?" I asked Jim as we wound our way out of the center of Bayonne. I was concerned because my husband and I have opposite approaches to travel. It's similar to our approach to cooking.: I follow directions and carefully measure ingredients. My husband glances at a recipe then, with total abandon, tosses in anything that resembles the required ingredients along with any spice within his reach. His meals are delicious.

"Did you check the map again before we left?" I ask, re-wording the first question.

Jim nods. "It's pretty straightforward," he responds nonchalantly.

"Here." With one hand on the wheel, he reaches with the other to grab the map in the back seat and tosses it on my lap.

Jim and I have been married for over four decades, and during those years I have proven to be completely incompetent when it comes to reading maps.

"Just look for the D932 and the D918 south to Saint-Jean-Pied-de-Port," Jim instructs. The print was minute. I fish my reading glasses out of my purse, but still cannot read the map.

"You need to pull over and see for yourself. You know I can't read maps," I whine.

I grew up in a small East Midlands town in England where things didn't change much. Directions to strangers went like this: "Turn right by the fish and chip shop, and left at Turnell's grocers." Even navigational guides like the sun rising in the East and setting in the West were not helpful for inhabitants of an island with perpetual cloud cover.

"Pauline, just find Bayonne, then look south and you'll see it. You can't miss it. I just want to make sure of the highway numbers."

I detect a rise in Jim's voice. With no help from me, we manage to drive directly into the town center of Saint-Jean-Pied-de-Port. Jim stops at the first intersection. We have no idea which way to turn. Jim edges the car closer to a wooden signpost. We look up at the sign and then turn to each other swapping looks of disbelief. The signpost reads "D301 Esterencuby," a town so small we'd been unable to find it on the local map.

Jim turns right and drives the car up the narrow road. He drives slowly enough to allow us to look down and admire the rolling green hills dotted with white-washed houses with red-tiled roofs, and windows boxes crammed with scarlet chrysanthemums.

Our stomachs remind us it is lunchtime. At first, we hesitate to pull into the parking area of the sprawling white stucco building with a Hotel Auberge Carricaburu sign. Scaffolding covers most of the building. Several middle-aged couples in hiking gear are seated at one of the outside tables so we assume the place is open.

No sooner have Jim and I planted ourselves on a picnic bench than a stout man with sparse dark hair emerges from a side door. His cheeks are bright red and his black eyebrows arch so high he looks surprised.

"Bonjour," he says and drops two large menus on the table, then leaves.

Neither of us can read our menu. We ask for help from the hiking couples, but they are German and don't speak French. They do understand English. We learn they are walking the trail to the Cathedral of Santiago de Compostela in northwestern Spain. I am impressed. These people must have been in their sixties. I'd seen the movie, "The Way," and knew this was an arduous trek, and that each year thousands of people from around the world attempt this pilgrimage.

Our server arrives with a carafe of red wine and two glasses. We point to our menu selection, try to get comfortable on the wooden bench, clink glasses, and soak in the bucolic surroundings. Before I take my second sip of wine two large platters are plunked down before us. I stifle a giggle until the waiter is out of earshot.

Jim had chosen a dish he thought included a juicy burger. He was staring at a plate of something neither of us recognized that was topped with a barely fried egg. Jim dove right in proving when you're hungry you'll eat anything.

After we finish our meal, Jim goes inside to pay the bill. He's smiling when he returns.

"You won't believe this, but I just met the wife of the waiter. She's my cousin."

While paying the bill, Jim asks the server, who owns the hotel and is named Michael, if he knows anyone in the town named Maitia, his grandfather's surname. A woman sitting nearby jumps up and loudly proclaims, "Moi Maitia!"

I follow Jim back inside the hotel. His new-found cousin rushes forward and huggs me. She looks about 40, petite and blonde. The light hair surprises me since most Basque have dark-hair. We struggle to understand each other.

I decide to phone our daughter, Tina, in California, who speaks fluent French.

Cousin Marie Agnes and Tina speake until the cell phone battery beeps a warning. Tina relays the names and contact numbers that Marie provides. While the telephone conversations are going on Jim has returned to our car and retrieves a photograph of Poppa's house. Michael nods in recognition. Using hand gestures, he indicates he will lead us to the house.

During the winding climb, Jim and I marvel at our luck in not only finding a cousin, but also one who can lead us to Poppa's house. There is a construction detour around almost every bend in the road. We would have gotten lost without a guide.

Michael pulls off the road across from a white-washed building similar in appearance to his hotel. Scrawled in decorative burgundy letters across the front of the building is "Les Sources de la Nive"—the source of the River Nive. We get out of our car and stand next to Michael. He points to a narrow trail with a sign indicating no cars allowed; we will have to make the rest of the journey on foot

"Merci beaucoup," we both call out to Michael as he turns to leave, showing off two of our seven words of French.

It is hot, and I am unprepared for the narrow, dusty and rocky trail. If this is a challenge, I thought, I cannot image hiking the 500 miles to the Cathedral of Santiago de Compostela. At least I am wearing sneakers, having chosen comfort over style that morning.

As we walk up the slight incline, Jim spots a red-tiled roof.

"There it is!" he shouts. When the building came into full view, we realize it is an abandoned stone barn.

"I'm going to tease you about this," I say as I snap a picture.

We see several more buildings.

"I think this is it," Jim says quietly as we stop by a large rock house. He pulls a piece of folded paper from his trouser pocket, and we study the scanned photograph.

"It *is* the house," I agree. "It looks like it has had some minor renovations, but look," I say, pointing first to the picture and then to the house, "it's the same roofline, same chimney, the same doorway and number of windows."

We walk further up the trail to look at the house from a different angle. There is a slow-moving stream running along the back of the property.

"To think," says my husband, "that when Poppa was a boy, he fished in this stream. It's the source of the River Nive that flows down to Bayonne. Look how much this area resembles Hope Valley and the West Carson River where Poppa immigrated when he was 16."

There's no wind to rustle the trees, only the soft gurgle of the stream. I reach for Jim's hand.

We walk back to the front of the house and contemplate knocking on the front door, but the gate is closed with a rope tied around the two posts. Jim reaches over the low rock wall and taps on a side window. Nobody answers.

We walk slowly back to our car.

"Do you know," Jim says, "that if we had continued up the trail, we would have reached Spain?"

****

Home

W e'd planned a visit to my hometown after our quest to find Poppa's house. After landing at London's Gatwick Airport we made our way via the tube to catch our train.

We arrived at London's Underground during rush hour, an experience I hope never to repeat. Masses of commuters packed shoulder to shoulder were exiting Paddington Station as Jim and I entered. An involuntary, "Oh sxxt," escaped when I saw this mob from the top of the platform steps. A loudspeaker ordered incoming travelers (us), to stay to the right in single file while the preferential hordes leaving the city moved as a single wave up towards us. There were so many people that a station attendant had to hold them back with an expandable gate, then let them through in phases.

When I had shared travel plans with my London-born friend, Irene, she'd warned me about rush hour in the tube. We were still surprised. By some miracle, we managed to squeeze onto a subway train that would transport us to St. Pancras Station, the East Midland's line to Wellingborough, my hometown.

Like a lot of London structures, St. Pancras railway station was built during Queen Victoria's reign. I had read it had the largest single-span roof in the world at the time, with magnificent arches. Unfortunately, the station had been allowed to deteriorate and there was the talk of demolishing it. Enough citizens were appalled by this suggestion that a campaign, led by Poet Laureate John Betjeman helped save St. Pancras. A seven-foot bronze statue was erected in his honor. "The statue stands on a disc of Cumbrian slate inscribed with Betjeman's name and dates and the words 'Who saved this glorious station.'"

I must have looked a little like the poet's statue which shows John Betjeman's head tilted back staring up in awe, as I turned in slow circles, admiring the renovations. Dazzled, I felt as if I had entered a futuristic space station—shining steel and gleaming glass. There was a modern shopping arcade and trendy little cafes—what a contrast from the sooty walls and smoky dives I remember as a teenager. St. Pancras International, as it's known, is now a hub for high-speed Eurostar trains zooming off to France and Brussels via the English Channel tunnel.

Coffee in hand, Jim and I boarded the East Midlands train to Wellingborough.

I'd booked three nights at the 17th century Hind Hotel in town. The building covers half a block at the crossroads of Sheep Street and Market Street— one end of a pedestrian-only town square. Although a majestic golden hind statue is mounted on the second story wooden porch above the hotel's entrance, I had no idea this female deer was the hotel's namesake. When growing up in Wellingborough, I was too young, and self-absorbed, to appreciate the history and architectural beauty of the building .

After checking in we quietly followed the receptionist through one of the long, narrow corridors. She unlocked the door of Room 107 and handed Jim the key.

I had stayed at the Hind on previous trips home. This was Jim's first stay and I had warned him that the elegant exterior did not transfer into an elegant interior, although I'd read they were renovating.

We entered a room that was surprisingly modern, and disappointedly modest. A double bed, covered by a faded bedspread, was pushed against one wall. The rest of the "furnishings" included a small television perched on a low table in front of the window and a chipped dressing table with a wood-framed mirror next to a narrow wardrobe. The place looked more like a cheap American motel room than an elegant English Carriage Inn.

The only attractive feature was the clean and spacious bathroom. I decided to focus on the positive and take a nice hot shower while Jim wrestled with the television. Believe me when I say "hot." I soon discovered why signs were posted warning guests about the temperature of the water. The shower operating instructions were in small print, and with no bathroom fan, my reading glasses fogged up. I barely escaped third-degree burns.

Weren't hotels supposed to run out of hot water? I persevered, showered, then flopped onto the bed and barely felt the lumps in the mattress.

We woke to a gloriously sunny morning. I was anxious to take a stroll around town. Sadly, my hometown bears little resemblance to the place where I grew up. Gone is The Lyric Cinema on Midland Road, a town fixture since 1936. This once grand place was where I and hordes of other kids in the late '40s and the '50s spent Saturday mornings laughing and yelling and screaming at cartoons and films. Wellingborough had four cinemas then: The Lyric, The Regal, the Silver, and the Palace. The Lyric was the last to go. Home videos were blamed, but it was the decision to build an indoor shopping mall on the site that reduced the Lyric to rubble in the 1970s.

The little zoo that once occupied a site on Sheep Street is gone. A plaque on a brick wall is all that remains of it. Few of the quaint shops that lined Sheep, Market, and Midland Roads exist, replaced by generic plate glass windows in the mall.

I've read that the crowds of people resettled from London in the 1960s—known as the London overspill, relocated to ease overcrowding in the capital city—had a detrimental effect on this once, small rural town. International trade deals also took a toll.

Wellingborough and the broader shire of Northampton were once thriving footwear manufacturers. One of my first jobs was working in a shoe factory and positions were so plentiful that I could hop from one factory to another without missing a day's work. Now I'm not sure if there's one shoe factory in Wellingborough.

Back at the hotel, we enjoyed visits in the upgraded bar with my two brothers, Kevan and Billy, niece Sarah, childhood friends Dawn, and Joy and her husband, Den. Another treat awaited us that evening when Kevan, his wife Heather, their son Asa, and friend, Roz, invited us for dinner at Heather's favorite restaurant in the village of Wadenhoe. The picturesque restaurant, the King's Head, a 17th century thatched-roof inn, overlooked the River Nene. We ambled in the meadows before dinner while Kevan's two dogs took a swim. This was picture-postcard England—thatched roofs, dark green meadows and a placid river.

After breakfast on our last morning in Wellingborough just as I was about to leave the café that adjoined the hotel, a woman approached me.

"Pauline?" she asked. I nodded, trying to recognize the face. "It's Jean Cripps. We used to live across the street from you." Then I remembered. I went to school with her brother Billy.

"Bill's in Australia. He isn't doing very well. I was there about a month ago. He has a Croyland Road School photo, and you're in it."

I offered my sympathies about her brother's condition and apologized for having to rush off—explaining the taxi was waiting.

"I don't use the computer," she said, "so I'll send you the photo."

We said our goodbyes promising to keep in touch. I relayed the conversation to Jim. I couldn't believe that I would be seeing a picture of myself as a child. I'd never seen a photograph where I was younger than age 15. When it was time to purchase school pictures my mother always said she knew what we all looked like. We knew she couldn't afford them.

True to her word, Jean Cripps sent me the school photograph. I looked at the two dark faces in the group and couldn't tell who was me, and who was my friend, Dawn. I scanned the picture and sent it to my daughter who immediately identified me as the one in the middle.

"You look just the same," she said.

The photograph became the cover for my memoir.

Postscript: The Hind Hotel is under new ownership, and undergoing restoration and renovation. I'm looking forward to staying there during my next trip to Wellingborough.

"FUDGE"

The Downs and Ups of a Biracial, Half-Irish
British War Baby

a memoir
Pauline Nevins

Available on Amazon and in bookstores

ABOUT THE AUTHOR

A group of American air force friends passed the hat around to fly Pauline and her two young children from a blustery British seaside town to New York City in 1970. Three days on a bus, decorated with a galloping dog, would get the young family from an abusive situation in England to California, and to a new love and a new life.

After 10 years of working and going to college part-time, Pauline earned a degree in Communication Studies, an unattainable dream for a working-class girl in England.

Years later, retirement afforded her the time to develop a passion for writing, something she never knew she had.

With encouragement from members of an informal writing group, Pauline authored a memoir in 2015: *"Fudge" The Downs and Ups of a Biracial, Half-Irish British War Baby,* and began publishing personal essays.

Following the publication of *Bonkers for Conkers* she's turned her focus to writing a first novel.

Pauline hopes that by publishing her life experiences she will encourage others to follow their interests, regardless of their age or circumstances.

"Who knows," Pauline says, "your interest may evolve into a passion, and enrich your life as writing has enriched mine."

Made in the USA
San Bernardino, CA
30 December 2018